E AFTER
SE SHEES

FRENCH

EXAM SUCCESS WITHOUT THE STRESS

Illustrated by Polly Dunbar

Rachel Wright is the author of over 20 books, many of them written for teenagers. She used to be an actress but is now a full-time writer. For Scholastic, she has also written *Reference Point: Sex* and *Dreadful Drama*.

Helen M. Wright, MA (Oxon), MA (Leics), PGCE, was the French adviser on this project. Helen teaches at Heathfield School Ascot.

With thanks to our consultants, Michelle Ogden and Julia Smart.

Scholastic Children's Books,
Commonwealth House, 1-19 New Oxford Street,
London, WC1A 1NU, UK
A division of Scholastic Ltd
London - New York - Toronto - Sydney - Auckland
Mexico City - New Delhi - Hong Kong

First published in the UK by Scholastic Ltd, 2001

Pour le plaisir verb exercises, *Manger: danger ou plaisir* and *La Drogue en France* are reproduced by permission of Mary Glasgow Magazines.

ISBN 0 439 01268 6

Typeset by M Rules
Printed by Cox & Wyman Ltd, Reading, Berks.

10 9 8 7 6 5 4 3 2 1

Contents

What is this book all about?

Wouldn't it be fabulous to be able to chat up a waiter or waitress in the south of France without the aid of suggestive sign language? To follow the plot of a classy French film without having to squint at the subtitles? To sail through your GCSE French course and exam, getting the highest grades you can?

> *Comment ça va, mon petit chou?* How's things, my little cabbage?

Sadly, this book can't guarantee that you'll get the date of your choice in France, or any date in any country for that matter, but it can act as a back-up to the teaching you're getting at school and help you firm up on any French grammar you're shaky on, greatly improve your reading, listening, writing and speaking skills, ensure any vocab you learn really does stick in your brain, and bump up your final exam grade from D/E to C or from C/B to A. What's more, it can help you do all this without boring you brain-dead in the process!

How you use the book will depend to some extent on what stage you are at in your course. For example, if your final exams are still a long way off, you probably won't need to bother with chapter 9 just yet (although you'll find the **Exam battle plans** in chapters 5–8 useful, as these tips about how to tackle exam questions apply to classwork too). For best results, you should read the book the whole way through (although probably not in one fell swoop!) and concentrate on those areas that are new to you or that you have covered in class but are still a bit wobbly about. Even if some of the information is really old ground as far as you are concerned, give it a quick read-through. You'd be amazed how many students keep making simple mistakes without realizing it because they are convinced that what they are writing or saying is right!

What did you say a verb was?

In a recent survey, nine out of a number of teenagers said they'd rather watch paint peel than learn French verbs.

If the mere mention of the word "verb" is enough to give you a headache, hold fire before you reach for the aspirin. OK, so swotting up on French verbs is not one of life's great pleasures, but it needn't be a torture. Provided you give yourself plenty of time to get fully to grips with all the information in this chapter and you don't try to learn too many verbs all at once, you shouldn't have any trouble at all. Trust me, I've got French A-level!

Verb profile

Let's start with a quick recap:
a verb is a word, or group of words,
that describe/s an action, e.g.

What **do** you **think**?

Your parents **are going to freak out** about this.

A lot of people get thrown by the idea that a verb can be made up of more than one word, so make sure you're not one of them.

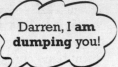

Darren, I **am dumping** you!

I **like** tall women!

Tense times

Verbs come in different tenses, the purpose of which is to describe *when* something happens, e.g.

past tense
(the "seeing" has happened)

past tense

Today I **saw** a purple-and-green sunset and **thought,** "Hey, I **am** colour-blind."

present tense

In French each tense has
six different verb endings, e.g.

Present tense of *regarder* – to watch
je regarde	I watch
tu regardes	you watch
il/elle regarde	he/she watches
nous regardons	we watch
vous regardez	you watch
ils/elles regardent	they watch

(For a quick run-down/reminder of the difference between *tu* and *vous*, see page 70. To find out the difference between *nous* and *on*, see page 72.)

Verbs are a <u>vital</u> part of a language so it's crucial that you know your French verb endings inside out. (If you don't believe that verbs are the big boys of the word world, try saying something meaningful in English without using a verb and see how far you get.) One easy way to familiarize yourself with French verb endings is to use the following **Verb guide** each time you need to find a verb form. The more you use the guide, the faster you'll become at discovering the correct form of the verb. In time, you should find you've practised so much, you've actually <u>memorized</u> the guide's step-by-step instructions. Once this happens, practise running through these instructions in your head until you are able to come up with the verb forms you want automatically.

If you want to practise using this guide on something other than your classwork or homework, you'll find some verb puzzles on pages 32–34.

Verb guide to help you find the right verb form in French

- Work out what you want to say in English.
- Decide **when** the action happened.
- Then follow the icon to the correct tense.

Present
If the action is happening now, or happens, turn to page 11 and find this shape:

Future
If the action *is going to* happen, turn to page 13 and find this shape:

If the action *will* happen, turn to page 14 and find this shape:

If the action *would* happen *if* something else happened, turn to page 27 and find this shape:

Past
If the action *was* happening, *used to* happen or happen*ed* regularly, turn to page 21 and find this shape:

If the action happened in the past and was a completed action, or happened only once, turn to page 16 and find this shape:

If the action *had* happened, turn to page 23 and find this shape:

Present tense

If the action you want to talk about is happening now or happens regularly or sometimes, you need to use the present tense, e.g.

Derek irons his anorak each morning.
Colette is hoovering the hamster.
Why do fools fall in ponds?

To find the correct form for the present tense . . .

1. Look up the verb you want in the dictionary. Remember, if you want to say something like "I am thinking", look up "think", not "am". In English, verbs have three forms of the present tense: "I think", "I am thinking", "I do think". In French, there is only one form (hurrah!): *je pense.*

2. The verb you look up in the dictionary will be in a neutral form known as the infinitive, e.g. *penser* – to think.

3. Check the verb lists on pages 198–210 to see if your verb is irregular or semi-regular. If it is, choose the form you need from the list and put the kettle on. Your search is at an end. If it's not irregular in any way . . .

4. . . . it must be regular. That means it must follow one of these patterns.

Verbs ending in **-er**	Verbs ending in **-ir**
Take off the **-er** and add	Take off the **-ir** and add
je ....*e*	je ....*is*
tu ....*es*	tu ....*is*
il/elle/on ....*e*	il/elle/on ....*it*
nous ....*ons*	nous ....*issons*
vous ....*ez*	vous ....*issez*
ils/elles ....*ent*	ils/elles ....*issent*

Verbs ending in -re
Take off the **-re** and add

je ....s
tu ....s
il/elle/on ....(nothing to add)
nous ....ons
vous ....ez
ils/elles ....ent

The less
I think, the
better I feel

5. End of search! Treat yourself to a cup of tea!

FANCY THAT!
Practically all verbs ending in **-er**, except *aller*, are regular.

TOP TIP
The French don't pronounce the **-ent** that comes at the end of the *ils/elles* form of present tense verbs, so for speaking purposes pretend it isn't there.

Future tense

If you want to talk about something that is going to happen, you need to use the present tense of the verb "to go" plus the infinitive of the verb you want, e.g.

(present tense of the verb "to go")

I am going to make a cup of tea.

(infinitive)

START HERE

1. Look up the verb you want in the dictionary. You'll find it ready and waiting in a neutral form known as the infinitive, e.g. *faire* – to make.

2. Put the infinitive after one of the following:

je	*vais**	<u>*faire*</u>		*nous*	*allons*	<u>*faire*</u>
tu	*vas*	<u>*faire*</u>		*vous*	*allez*	<u>*faire*</u>
il/elle/on	*va*	<u>*faire*</u>		*ils/elles*	*vont*	<u>*faire*</u>

* Vais, vas, va, etc. are the present tense of the verb *aller* – to go.

> *L'année prochaine, je vais passer mes vacances en Ibiza sans mes parents.*

3. End of search!

Future tense

If you want to talk about something that will or shall happen, you need the future tense, e.g.

> You **shall go** to the ball, Cinderella!
> **Will** you still **love** me next Tuesday?
> When you **finish** this book, you **will be** much brainier.

(i.e. the "finishing" of this book has yet to happen and so is in the future!)

1. Look up the verb you want in the dictionary. You'll find it in a neutral form known as the infinitive, e.g. *travailler* – "to work".

2. Check the list on pages 198–210 to see if your verb is an irregular one, or a semi-regular one with an odd future form. If it is either of these, copy the verb form you need and treat yourself to a French Fancy. Your search is at an end. If it isn't an irregular verb . . .

3. . . . it must be a regular one. In which case, add one of the following endings to the infinitive of the verb. (If the infinitive ends in **-re**, drop the final **-e** before adding one of these endings.)

> *je* ....*ai*
> *tu* ....*as*
> *il/elle/on* ....*a*
> *nous* ....*ons*
> *vous* ....*ez*
> *ils/elles* ....*ont*

4. End of search!

FANCY THAT!
The endings of the future tense are almost the same as the present tense of *avoir* – to have. Not bad, eh? Only one set of endings to learn for two tenses.

Samedi prochain vous gagnerez beaucoup d'argent. Vous abandonnerez votre travail dans un supermarché et vous habiterez un centre commercial où vous passerez votre temps à dépenser de l'argent.

Perfect tense

If you want to talk about something that has happened and is now complete, you need to use the perfect tense. In English, this tense can have one or two parts, e.g.

I **danced**¹ with a disco diva.

I **have**¹ **danced**² with a disco diva.

In French, the perfect tense always has two parts – the present tense of the verbs *avoir* or *être*, and a past participle.

To form the perfect tense . . .

1. Look up the verb you want in the dictionary. You'll find it in a form known as the infinitive, e.g. *danser* – to dance.

2. Check to see whether it's an ADVENT verb (see page 211) or a reflexive verb (does it have *se* or *s'* in front of it like *se laver*?). If it is neither of these, skip to step **5.** If it <u>is</u> one of these, the first part of the perfect tense will be made up of the present tense of *être* –

je	*suis*
tu	*es*
il/elle/on	*est*
nous	*sommes*
vous	*êtes*
ils/elles	*sont*

– and the second part will be the past participle.

The past participle of ADVENT verbs is given in brackets on page 211, e.g.

> *Il est **sorti** et je suis **descendu(e)**.*
> **He went out and I came down.**

The past participle of irregular reflexive verbs is underlined in the irregular verb list on pages 201–210, e.g.

> *Il s'est **assis**.*
> **He sat down.**

 To form the past participle of <u>regular</u> reflexive verbs, take the infinitive, drop the **-er/-ir/-re** from the end and add . . .

-é to **-er** verbs
-i to **-ir** verbs
-u to **-re** verbs.

> *David s'est **lavé**.*
> **David washed himself.**

3. Check to see whether the person/thing that did the action is feminine. If it is, add **-e** to the end of the past participle. For more about the gender of words in French, see page 36.

> *La voiture est **arrivée**.*
> **The car arrived.**

If more than one thing/person did the action, add **-s**.

> *Les garçons sont **restés**.*
> **The boys stayed.**

And if the people/things that did the action are all feminine, add **-es** instead.

> *Les filles sont descendues.*
> **The girls came down.**

When talking about a mixed group of males and females, put your feminist principles on hold and use the <u>masculine</u> plural spelling of the past participle, e.g.

> *Jack et Jill sont **tombés** dans le puits.*
> **Jack and Jill fell in the well.**

4. End of search.

TOP TIP

If you're a girl and you want to talk about what you have done or did using an *être* verb, remember to add an extra -e to the past participle.

"Je suis née en 1907," a dit Sophie.
"I was born in 1907," said Sophie.

5. If it isn't an ADVENT verb or a reflexive verb, the first part will be made up of the present tense of *avoir* –

j'*	*ai*	*nous*	*avons*
tu	*as*	*vous*	*avez*
il/elle/on	*a*	*ils/elles*	*ont*

– and the second part will be the past participle. Check pages 201–210 to see if your verb is irregular. If it is, copy down the past participle (the word underlined) and put your feet up. If it isn't an irregular verb . . .

6. . . . it must be a regular one! To form the past participle of regular verbs, take the infinitive, drop the **-er/-ir/-re** from the end and add . . .

> -é to **-er** verbs
> -i to **-ir** verbs
> -u to **-re** verbs.

7. End of search!

* *je* becomes *j'* when used before a vowel.

Secret thoughts of the examiner

If you want to send your grade into the stratosphere, check out the following carefully and use what you learn in your writing:

In general, verbs that form the perfect tense with *avoir* don't add -e, -s or -es to the past participle, regardless of whether the *elle*, *nous*, *vous*, *ils* or *elles* form of the verb is being used. HOWEVER . . . (and this is a big "however") . . . if you want to form a sentence in which a feminine or plural direct object* comes before an *avoir* verb, you have to add -e, -s or -es on to the end of the past participle.

direct object/plural   past participle

*Voici **les concombres** que j'ai achetés.*
Here are the cucumbers I bought.

direct object/feminine past participle

*Voici ma **sœur** – je **l**'ai **vue** ce matin.*
Here's my sister – I saw her this morning.

*If you've no idea what the subject of a sentence is, let alone the direct object, stay calm. The subject is the most important thing/person in a sentence because it is the doer of the verb. The direct object is the second most important thing/person in a sentence because it is closely related to the subject. And while we're in this groove, the indirect object is the third most important thing/person in a sentence and is the furthest removed from the subject, e.g.

Elroy sent **a sack of snails** to **his mother-in-law**.

1. subject   2. direct object   3. indirect object

Imperfect tense

If you want to describe something that was happening at some point or used to happen in the past, you need the imperfect tense.

In English you need two or even three words to form the imperfect tense, e.g.

>   1   2
>
> I **was driving** my mum's car when I crashed into a creep.

>   1   2   3
>
> I **used to drive** to school by car.

>   1   2 3
>
> I **used to be** my mum's favourite son.

In French, being imperfect is much easier because you only need one word.

1. Look up the verb you want in the dictionary. You'll find it in a form known as the infinitive, e.g. *conduire* – to drive.

2. Work out the *nous* form of the present tense, e.g. *nous conduisons*. (See page 11 if you need help working this out.)

3. Take off the **-ons** and add

je.................*ais*		*nous*..............*ions*	
tu ....*ais*		*vous*..............*iez*	
il/elle/on ......*ait*		*ils/elles* ....*aient*	

4. End of search!

Believe it or not, there is only really one important verb – *être* (to be) – that doesn't form the imperfect tense in the usual way. Its endings are the same as those on page 21, but the main part of the verb, or stem, doesn't use the *nous* form of the present tense.

j'étais	I was	nous étions	we were
tu étais	you were	vous étiez	you were
il/elle était	he/she/it was	ils/elles étaient	they were

Manger and *lancer* have a couple of slightly odd imperfect forms too, so don't forget to check them out on pages 199 and 200.

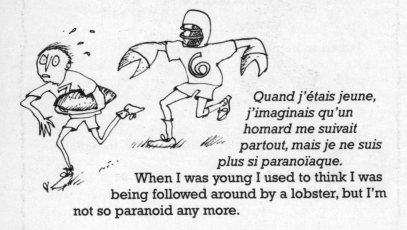

Quand j'étais jeune, j'imaginais qu'un homard me suivait partout, mais je ne suis plus si paranoïaque.
When I was young I used to think I was being followed around by a lobster, but I'm not so paranoid any more.

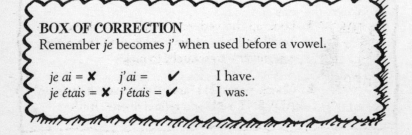

BOX OF CORRECTION
Remember *je* becomes *j'* when used before a vowel.

je ai = ✗	j'ai = ✔	I have.
je étais = ✗	j'étais = ✔	I was.

Pluperfect tense

If you want to talk about the past before the past, i.e. something that had happened before something else happened, you need to use the pluperfect tense.

the past

Sally was beginning to regret that she had picked her spot before her date.

the past before the past

1. Look up the verb you want in the dictionary. You'll find it in a form known as the infinitive, e.g. *gratter* – to scratch, to pick.

2. Check pages 211 and 195 to see if it is an ADVENT verb or a reflexive one. If it's

23

neither, skip to step **5.** If it <u>is</u> either, the first part of the pluperfect tense will be made up of the imperfect tense of *être* –

j'	étais	nous	étions
tu	étais	vous	étiez
il/elle/on	était	ils/elles	étaient

– and the second part will be the past participle.

The past participle of ADVENT verbs is given in brackets on page 211, e.g.

> *J'étais **allé(e)** au cinéma.*
> I had gone to the cinema.

> *Il était **arrivé** au cinéma.*
> He had arrived at the cinema.

The past participle of irregular reflexive verbs is underlined in the irregular verb list on pages 201–210, e.g.

> *Il s'était **assis**.*
> He had sat down.

To form the past participle of <u>regular</u> reflexive verbs, take the infinitive, drop the **-er/-ir/-re** from the end and add . . .

> **-é** to **-er** verbs
> **-i** to **-ir** verbs
> **-u** to **-re** verbs.

> *David s'était **habillé**.*
> David had got dressed.

3. Check to see whether the person/thing that had done the action is feminine.* If it is, add **-e** to the end of the past participle.

La voiture était partie.
The car had gone.

If more than one thing/person had done the action, add **-s**.

Les garçons étaient arrivés.
The boys had arrived.

And if the people/things that had done the action are all feminine, add **-es** instead.

Les filles étaient descendues.
The girls had come down.

When talking about a mixed group of males and females, remember to use the <u>masculine</u> plural spelling of the past participle, e.g.

Jack et Jill étaient tombés dans le puits.
Jack and Jill had fallen in the well.

*For more about the gender of words in French, see page 36.

4. End of search. If you got through all that without a hitch, you deserve *un congé* – a day off work!

5. If it isn't an ADVENT verb or a reflexive verb, the first part of the pluperfect tense will be made up of the imperfect tense of *avoir* –

j'	*avais*	*nous*	*avions*
tu	*avais*	*vous*	*aviez*
il/elle/on	*avait*	*ils/elles*	*avaient*

– and the second part will be the past participle. Check pages 201–210 to see whether your verb's on the irregular list. If it is, copy down the past participle (the word underlined) and call it a day.

6. If it isn't an irregular verb, it must be a regular one! To form the past participle of regular verbs, take the infinitive, drop the **-er/-ir/-re** from the end and add . . .

-**é** to **-er** verbs
-**i** to **-ir** verbs
-**u** to **-re** verbs.

7. End of search!

Quand je suis arrivé(e) à l'école, la première leçon avait commencé.
When I arrived at school, the first lesson had started.

Conditional tense

If you want to say something that has an element of possibility about it, you need to use the conditional tense, e.g.

I would speak to you if you weren't such a scumbag! If I won the lottery I wouldn't study.

START HERE **1.** Look up the verb you want in the dictionary. You'll find it in a form known as the infinitive, e.g. *parler* – to speak.

2. Check pages 198–210 to see if your verb is semi-regular or irregular. If it's semi-regular with a spelling change in the conditional tense, copy whichever form of the verb you need and make some French toast. Your search is at an end. If it's irregular, copy down the main part of the verb <u>in the future tense</u> minus any ending, e.g. **ir-** for the verb *aller*, **aur-** for the verb *avoir*, then add the appropriate ending from step **3** below. If your verb isn't irregular in any way . . .

3. . . . add one of the following endings to the infinitive. (If the infinitive ends in **-re**, drop the final **-e** before adding one of these endings.)

je ....*ais*		*nous* ....*ions*	
tu ....*ais*		*vous* ....*iez*	
il/elle/on ....*ait*		*ils/elles* ....*aient*	

4. End of search!

If the endings given in step **3** look familiar, it's because they are the same endings as those used in the imperfect tense. Good stuff, eh? Only one set of endings to learn for two whole tenses!

Cher Robbie Williams,
Je voudrais poser ma candidature pour le poste de ta petite amie.

Dear Robbie Williams,
I would like to apply for the job as your girlfriend.

Reflecting on reflexives

Dowdy Dion
Agony Aunt
Miel Magazine
Rue du Rhum
Montpellier

Dear Dowdy,

My mate says that reflexive verbs are nothing but ordinary verbs with a bit extra thrown in at the start. Can this be true? I always thought they were incredibly complicated little *@!!!*s and best left well alone. Which of us is right?

    Delbert

Delbert Sharp
666 Devils Gate Drive
High Wycombe

Cher Delbert,
Your mate eez right! Reflexive verbs are indeed simply ordinary verbs wiz a bit extra thrown in at ze start. Regardez . . .

extra bit
↓
se réveiller – to wake up

extra bit
↓
se laver – to wash

s'habiller – to get dressed
↑
extra bit

se lever – to get up
↑
extra bit

Zis extra bit shouldn't drive you krezzy though because eet follows an easy-to-remember pattern.

je **me** réveille	I wake up (literally, I wake myself up)
tu **te** réveilles	you wake up
il **se** réveille	he wakes up
elle **se** réveille	she wakes up
on **se** réveille	we/they wake up
nous **nous** réveillons	we wake up
vous **vous** réveillez	you wake up
ils **se** réveillent	they wake up
elles **se** réveillent	they wake up

Ze main thing to remember about reflexive verbs eez zat zey take "être" in ze perfect and pluperfect tenses, e.g.

Je me suis levé(e) à sept heures.
I got up at seven o'clock.

And if zey refer to somezing female or somezing plural in ze perfect or pluperfect tenses, ze past participle of the verb as to agree with ze elle, il, ils, etc., e.g.

Elle s'est couchée tard.
She went to bed late.

Elles s'étaient souvenues d'acheter des baskets.
They had remembered to buy some trainers.

So, as you can see, Delbert, ze reflexive verbs are nothing to run scared of (which eez more than can be said of your British drivers)!

Amitiés,
Dowdy

P.S. Did you notice that ze endings for reflexive verbs follow the normal patterns? Fantastique, huh?

Secret thoughts of the examiner

If we GCSE examiners had to list the verbs we most love to hear or see used correctly, *pouvoir* – to be able, *vouloir* – to want, wish, and *devoir* – to have to, to owe, "must", would make it into our top ten. These three verbs, which are usually followed by the infinitive of another verb, are listed in the irregular verb list (pages 201–210), so make sure you get to know them inside out!

> *Pourriez-vous me dire l'heure, s'il vous plaît?*
> **Could you tell me the time please?**

Precise meaning:
Would you be able to tell me the time, please?

> *Je sais...*
> **I know...**

> *Tu devrais ranger ta chambre plus souvent, tu sais ...*
> **You ought to tidy your room more often, you know ...**

(The conditional of *devoir* means "ought to".)

Je veux ma maman!
I want my mummy!

TOP TIP
One way to learn verb endings is to chant them to yourself and spell them out loud whenever you can. In time they will sink into your long-term memory, alongside other valuable information you've got stored there such as when Michael Owen first played footie for England and who's who in *Neighbours*.

Pour le plaisir! (For fun!)
OK! Be honest. How much of all that you've read about verbs has <u>really</u> sunk in? Everything? Nothing at all? Here's your chance to find out.

1. Complete this story by putting all the verbs in brackets in the imperfect or perfect tense (see pages 21 and 16).

Je .... (regarder) la télévision quand mon père .... (téléphoner). Il .... (vouloir) parler à ma mère. Comme elle .... (prendre) un bain, elle .... (sortir) en vitesse, elle .... (mettre) un peignoir et elle .... (répondre) au téléphone. Mon père .... (dire) qu'il .... (aller) rentrer tard car il .... (avoir) beaucoup de travail. Ma mère .... (voir) que j' .... (être) déçu car c' .... (être) mon anniversaire. Alors, elle m' .... (inviter) au restaurant.

2. Complete this story by putting all the verbs in brackets in the future tense (see page 14).

Demain, j' .... (avoir) dix-sept ans. Ma mère .... (acheter) un grand gâteau au chocolat! Mes amis me .... (donner) beaucoup de cadeaux. L'après-midi, nous .... (aller) au cinéma et le soir, nous .... (faire) une grande fête chez moi. Ce .... (être) super! Il y .... (avoir) tous mes amis! Le seul problème, c'est Marc. Il ne .... (pouvoir) pas venir parce qu'il travaille, mais il me .... (téléphoner), il me l'a promis.

3. Complete this bit of wishful thinking by putting all the verbs in brackets in the conditional tense (see page 27).

Si j'étais très riche, j' .... (acheter) une grande maison avec une piscine. Je .... (faire) le tour du monde. Je .... (visiter) le plus de pays possible et j' .... (inviter) mes amis. Nous .... (s'amuser) beaucoup! Mes parents, eux, ... (recevoir) une voiture comme cadeau et ma petite sœur .... (avoir) tous les jouets qu'elle .... (vouloir).

4. Complete this holiday write-up by putting all the verbs in brackets in the imperfect or perfect tense (see pages 21 and 16).

L'année dernière, je .... (aller) *en Martinique. J'y ....* (rester) *trois semaines. J' ....* (avoir) *de la chance parce que c' ....* (être) *la période du carnaval. J' ....* (voir) *tous les défilés. Il y ....* (avoir) *du monde partout. Les groupes de musique ....* (jouer) *de la musique fantastique. Les gens ....* (danser) *et ....* (chanter). *Il y ....* (avoir) *une ambiance super.*

5. Complete these sentences by putting the verbs in brackets into the pluperfect tense (see page 23).

● *Pour réaliser son film* **Le Grand Bleu**, *le réalisateur Luc Besson ....* (s'inspirer) *des exploits de Jacques Mayol, le célèbre plongeur français.*

● *Si seulement l'équipe anglaise ....* (gagner) *la coupe du monde 1998!*

● *William et Wilma ont dit qu'ils ....* (aller) *à la discothèque avec leurs amis.*

Answers on page 212.

If you fancy giving your brain a bit more to do, why not have a go at translating the questions above into English? If you get stuck, you can always sneak a look at the translations on page 215. Then why not translate them back to French without looking at the original exercise? This will really show that you know your stuff!

I can't make sense of French sentences!

Qu'est-ce que c'est le French for "Help"?

OK. So you may know the French for "I will snog" and "He should have scored", but if you don't know how to pad out your sentences with correctly spelt/pronounced nouns, adjectives, adverbs or pronouns, you'll soon come a cropper. Luckily, in this chapter you'll find all the essential information you need about words other than verbs. If you work your way through the chapter bit by bit, learning or brushing up on the rules as you go, you should end up with a firm enough grasp of French grammar to get you through your GCSE course and exams successfully. Remember, even if you think you already know everything there is to know about how to put sentences together in French, have a read through. You could be continually making simple errors and never checking them out because you're convinced you are right!

Checking out nouns!

Let's start with a recap: a noun is a word, or words, that refer(s) to a thing or a person. That thing or person can be something concrete, such as a "ladder" or a "loo roll", or it can be something abstract such as "embarrassment".

For some reason best known to the French, all French nouns have a gender, i.e. all of them are either masculine or feminine. The upshot of this is that you have to put *le* or *un* (the masculine forms of "the" or "a") in front of masculine singular nouns and *la* or *une* (the feminine forms of "the" or "a") in front of feminine singular nouns.

> *Vous êtes **une** poupée!*
> You are a babe!
>
> *Et vous êtes **un** cochon!*
> And you are a pig!

The word *l'* is used instead of *le* or *la* when the first letter of the noun is a vowel (**a**, **e**, **i**, **o**, **u**) or, sometimes, **h**.

Unfortunately the gender of French nouns is often far from obvious. (Can you think of any logical reason why a bra should be masculine but a banana feminine?) This means it's <u>vital</u> when learning a French noun to learn its gender at the same time. One way to help yourself remember the gender is to group masculine nouns together in one set of lists and feminine nouns together in another set of lists and learn nouns of one gender one day and the other gender the next. Alternatively, you could try thinking about masculine nouns in blue and feminine nouns in red when you learn them and see if that helps.

How do you du?

Like *le/la* and *un/une*, the French for "some" and "any" also have different spellings depending on the noun that follows. If you want to say "some/any" + a masculine singular noun, you put *du* (*de + le = du*) or *de l'* in front of the noun. And if you want to say "some/any" + a feminine singular noun, you use *de la* or *de l'* instead. If you are talking about some thing<u>s</u>, it is easy – use *des* whether the things are masculine or feminine.

> *Avez-vous du bandage élastique, s'il vous plaît? Je voudrais aussi de l'aspirine et de la pommade antiseptique ...*
> Have you any elastic bandage please? I'd also like some asprin and some antiseptic cream ...

If you want to say what you haven't got, in the negative, however, you use *de* instead of *du*, *de la*, e.g.

> *Je n'ai pas **de** fromage.*
> I haven't any cheese.

> *Il ne veut pas **de** café.*
> He doesn't want any coffee.

(For more about *ne . . . pas* and other negatives, see page 95.)

The only tricky thing about *du/de la/de l'* is that these words are often used in French where they wouldn't be in English. For example, if a gunman stormed into a newsagents in Britain shouting "Give me chocolate!", no one would fret about his grammar. But if he yelled "*Donnez-moi chocolat!*" instead of "*Donnez-moi du chocolat!*", French eyebrows would be raised. So, be warned: you have to think carefully about the <u>precise</u> meaning of what you want to say before translating into French.

Perfect plurals

More often than not, if you want to make a French noun plural all you have to do is add -s to the end of the noun and put *les* (the plural of *le* or *la*) or *des* (*de* + *les*), which means "any" or "some", in front of the noun, e.g.

l'élève	the pupil
les élèves	the pupils
un élève	a pupil
des élèves	some pupils

Again, if you want to say what you haven't got, use *de* instead of *des*, e.g.

Je n'ai pas eu de problèmes avec ce livre.
I haven't had any problems with this book.

The French don't usually pronounce the last consonant of a word so it's *très important* to listen out for/say the *le/la/les* or *un/une/des* as these words let everyone know whether the noun is in the plural.

So far so good? *Bon!* Because now comes the annoying part. There are several noun plurals that aren't formed by adding -s to the end.

AAAARGH!

You should be able to find most of these irregular plurals in your French/English dictionary, so if you learn them as you come across them during your course, you'll have one thing less to revise for your final exams. (See pages 102 and 103 to find out how to recognize irregular plurals in your dictionary.)

However, if you like rules, and want a few about irregular plurals, here are three to keep you going!

- Nouns that end in **-s**, **-x**, or **-z** make no change in the plural:

le bras	*les bras*	arm/s
la noix	*les noix*	nut/s

- Nouns that end in **-al** often form the plural by adding **-aux**.

le journal	*les journaux*	newspaper/s

(The common exceptions here are *le festival/les festivals* – festival/s *un bal/les bals* – ball/s.)

- Nouns that end in **-au** or **-eau** and most that end in **-eu** form the plural by adding **-x**.

le feu	*les feux*	fire/s
le bateau	*les bateaux*	boat/s

(Common exception: *un pneu/les pneus* – tyre/s.)

There are a few nouns that have plurals so irregular they have to be seen to be believed, e.g.

l'œil	*les yeux*	eye/s
le grand-père	*les grands-pères*	grandfather/s
le genou	*les genoux*	knee/s

. . . but you'll discover more about the common ultra-irregular plurals on page 102.

There are also a few nouns that when you add -s to the end mean something completely different (why, we ask ourselves?) . . . but the list isn't long:

> *une vacance* – a vacancy
> *les vacances* – holidays
> *un devoir* – a duty
> *les devoirs* – homework
> *un ciseau* – a chisel
> *les ciseaux* – scissors

TOP TIP

Don't get hung up on irregular noun plurals. If you don't know whether a noun has an irregular plural and you can't check in your dictionary, take a gamble and add -s. It usually works!

PETIT TEST

Give your grey matter a quick workout with this *petit* test.

1. Which word in each of these two lists is the odd one out because of its gender?

    a) *salle, église, griffe, passage, glace, page*
    b) *été, café, marché, moitié, immigré*

2. What are the plurals of these words?

un oiseau	des	*un feu*	des ....
un animal	des	*un pneu*	des ....
un fils	des	*un œuf*	des ....
une voix	des	*une plage*	des ....

3. Complete this letter to a French pen pal by choosing one of the words from this list. Use each word once and once only!

un, l', de la, de l', une, la, du, les, un, des

Salut

Je m'appelle Jackie. J'ai quinze ans et j'adore regarder ...... télé tous les jours. Mon émission préférée c'est ...... feuilleton. C'est ...... histoire de plusieurs familles à Manchester. ...... familles passent beaucoup de temps dans ...... bar. Quelle vie!

Hier matin ma télé est tombée en panne donc je suis allée en ville. J'ai rencontré ...... amies et nous avons fait les magasins. J'ai acheté ...... parfum et ma meilleure amie a acheté ...... crème pour les mains et ...... huile solaire.

Tu peux m'envoyer ...... photo de toi?

À bientôt

Jackie

Answers on page 216.

Sussing out adjectives

Let's start with a quick recap: an adjective is a word that describes a noun or defines it in some way:

> **Spotty** face?
> **Hideous** hair?
> Don't let **unattractive** adjectives ruin your appearance.

In French, most adjectives come after the noun, not before as in English.

> *Vous avez le visage **boutonneux**? Les cheveux **affreux**? Ne permettez pas aux adjectifs **déplaisants** de ruiner votre aspect!*

Now, for the tricky part! Unlike English adjectives, the French variety have different endings depending on the noun they describe.

WHAAAT???

In other words, if the noun is masculine singular, the adjective needs a masculine singular ending; if the noun is feminine singular, the adjective needs a feminine singular ending; and if the noun is masculine plural or feminine plural, the adjective needs a masculine or feminine plural ending. This is called making the adjective "agree with" the noun.

Five things you need to know about adjectives

1. The masculine singular form of an adjective is what you find in your bilingual dictionary, e.g. *un chien animé* – a lively dog.

2. To create the feminine singular of most adjectives, you add **-e** to the end of the dictionary spelling, e.g. *une discussion animée* – a lively conversation.

3. To create the masculine plural, you add **-s** to the dictionary spelling, e.g. *deux extra-terrestres animés* – two lively aliens.

4. To create the feminine plural, you add **-es**, e.g. *des religieuses animées* – some lively nuns.

If the masculine singular already ends in **-e** (without an accent), the feminine plural will just add **-s**.

"Give-me strength!"

There are some exceptions to these spelling patterns (*quelle surprise!*) that you should learn as you come across them in your coursebook and/or your bilingual dictionary. If you're not sure how to recognize irregular adjectives in your dictionary, check out page 102.

Talking of exceptions, there are also a number of common adjectives that go before the noun . . .

Adjectives that go in front of the noun

*beau**	beautiful, handsome	*joli*	pretty
*bon**	good	*long**	long
court	short	*mauvais*	bad
*gros**	big, fat	*même*	same
grand	tall	*haut*	high
jeune	young	*vieux**	old
petit	small		

For a list of other common adjectives that come before the noun, look on page 47! See page 103 for more about *beau* and *vieux* too.

* The adjectives marked with an asterisk all have irregular feminine spellings that you should look up in your dictionary and memorize! Once you've sussed them out, test yourself by reading this *carte postale* and making the adjectives agree with their nouns.

CHER JACQUES,

ME VOICI EN VACANCES À BOGNOR REGIS. HIER, J'AI FAIT LA CONNAISSANCE D'UNE JOLI JEUNE FEMME QUI S'APPELLE MONICA. ELLE A LES CHEVEUX BRUN ET LES YEUX BLEU ET LES PIEDS PARFAIT. ENSEMBLE, ON A VISITÉ LA VIEUX VILLE CE MATIN. APRÈS CELA, NOUS SOMMES ALLÉS AU CINÉMA ET NOUS AVONS REGARDÉ UN LONG FILM ANGLAISE SANS SOUS-TITRES QUE JE NE POUVAIS PAS COMPRENDRE. LA GRAMMAIRE ANGLAIS ME SEMBLE TRÈS DIFFICILE. SI SEULEMENT J'ÉTAIS BILINGUE!

À BIENTÔT,

MATT

Answers on page 216.

45

TOP TIP

If you want to say what something is made of, use *de* + the material, or in some cases, *en* + the material.

une jambe en bois   a wooden leg
un rideau de dentelle   a lace curtain
un sac en plastique   a plastic bag

Schizophrenic adjectives

If you think it is ridiculous and, quite frankly, unbelievable that you are expected to know one irregular French adjective, let alone the list on page 45, you may need to be sedated for the following.

There are a handful of adjectives in French that change their meaning, depending on whether they are used before or after the noun.

As luck would have it, a list of these adjectives appears next!

Adjective	Meaning before noun	Meaning after noun
ancien	former/ex *un ancien élève*	old/ancient *un élève ancien*
brave	good *un brave homme*	brave *un homme brave*
cher	dear/cherished *un cher ami*	expensive *un bijou cher*
dernier	last (of a series) *le dernier biscuit*	last (most recent) *la semaine dernière*
nouveau	new (fresh) *un nouveau rouleau de papier*	new (novel) *une idée nouvelle*
pauvre	poor (piteous) *un pauvre enfant*	poor (no money) *une famille pauvre*
prochain	next or nearest *la prochaine réunion*	next (the one after this one) *l'année prochaine*
propre	own *ma propre voiture*	clean *ma voiture propre*
seul	single/only *le seul candidat*	alone *un homme seul*
vrai	real/true *un vrai ami*	true (factual) *une histoire vraie*

PETIT TEST

So! You've checked out French adjectives and you think you've got them well and truly sussed! But have you? Try this *petit* test to find out:

1. On holiday in France, you spot a woman with a fried egg on her head peering through your hotel window. In your statement to the police, do you describe the woman as. . .
   a) *une personne bizarre?*
   b) *une bizarre personne?*
   c) your mother?

2. You are pushing your baby brother around a French supermarket when suddenly you notice that he has grabbed a packet of sanitary towels from the shelf and is sticking them all over his head. Do you. . .
   a) go red and call him *"un garçon mauvais"*?
   b) go red and call him *"un mauvais garçon"*?
   c) go red and hand him in at the nearest lost property desk?

3. At a cocktail party in Cannes you are chatted up by a crusty old bloke who describes himself as *"un ancien ami de Steven Spielberg"*. Desperate to make a name for yourself in the film business, do you. . .
   a) agree to meet him later for dinner in the hope he'll introduce you to Mr Spielberg?
   b) agree to marry him in the hope Mr Spielberg will be at the wedding?
   c) tell him you've got a nasty rash in the hope he'll go away?

4. A gorgeous French girl/lad takes you to *"un restaurant cher"* that s/he knows. At the end of the meal the waiter hands you the bill. Do you. . .

a) offer to pay the total without even looking at it. After all, you only had a main course each?

b) look at the total and suggest going Dutch?

c) shout "fire" and leg it to the door?

5. You are covering a story for *Le Daily Flash* about a team of firefighters who rescued a cat from a tree, then jumped back into their fire engine and ran over the cat by mistake. Anxious not to upset the cat's owner, do you describe the poor dead creature as. . .

a) *le chat pauvre?*

b) *le pauvre chat qui est mort?*

c) *le pauvre chat qui était horriblement écrasé?*

Answers on page 217.

Adverbs exposed!

Let's start with a recap: an adverb is a word that adds to a verb, i.e. it tends to describe how, when or where an action is done.

The clock on the mantelpiece chimed loudly.
The man in pink pyjamas left yesterday.
Do you come here often?

In French, many adverbs are formed by adding **-ment** to the feminine singular spelling of an adjective.

Adjective (fem. sing.)	Adverb	English
mystérieuse	*mystérieusement*	mysteriously
heureuse	*heureusement*	happily

49

HOWEVER . . .
. . . if the masculine singular form of the adjective ends in a vowel,
-ment is added on to that:

Adjective (masc. sing.)	Adverb	English
vrai	*vraiment*	truly
absolu	*absolument*	absolutely

And if the masculine singular form of the adjective ends in **-ant**
or **-ent**, the adverb ends in **-amment** or **-emment**:

Adjective (masc. sing.)	Adverb	English
courant	*couramment*	fluently
évident	*évidemment*	obviously

Odd one out:

lent	*lentement*	slowly

Now, if you've learnt anything about French grammar, it should
come as no surprise to you to learn that there are a few adverbs
that deviate from the general rules so outrageously, you wonder
what the French were thinking of when they dreamt them up!
Unfortunately, these rogue adverbs are used a lot, so make sure
you're on familiar terms with the following:

bien	well	*fort*	strong, loud
mal	badly	*gentiment*	kindly
souvent	often	*partout*	everywhere
tôt	early	*vite*	quickly
quelquefois	sometimes	*loin*	far
brièvement	briefly	*tard*	late

50

Adverbs à-go-go

Generally speaking, French adverbs go after the verb they describe/add to.

*Ma sœur regarde **souvent** la télé.*
My sister often watches TV.

*Mrs Bloggins est entrée **très doucement.***
Mrs Bloggins came in very quietly.

Short adverbs, however, usually go in front of a past participle or an infinitive.

*Antoine? Pah! Je l'ai **déjà** oublié.*
Antoine? Pah! I have forgotten him already.

Don't worry if you forget to put short adverbs in front of a past participle/infinitive and longer adverbs after. This is not a hard and fast rule, more a general guideline.

Four facts you never knew about tout

1. *Tout* can mean "all", "altogether" or "quite".

2. It can be used as an adjective as well as an adverb.

3. When used as an adverb before an adjective, *tout* agrees with the adjective only if it is feminine and begins with a consonant, e.g.

> *Cecile est toute seule.*
> Cecile is all alone.

4. When used as an adjective, however, *tout* agrees with every gender and number of noun going! (See page 112.)

PETIT TEST

To find out whether you've truly taken on board everything
you've read so far, try and do the following.

1. Match each adverb in column **A** with its opposite in
column **B**.

A	**B**
toujours	*peu*
vite	*cruellement*
très	*malheureusement*
souvent	*lentement*
heureusement	*rarement*
gentiment	*jamais*

2. Spot the common mistake in this newsflash.

*Hier soir, Jean Julliano, le créateur branché de la haute
couture française, est mort dans un accident de moto à
Walton-on-the-Naze. Bien que les circonstances exactes
de l'accident ne soient pas entièrement claires, il ne fait
aucun doute que Monsieur Julliano avait conduit trop
vitement.*

Mini word kit
branché(e) . . . trendy

3. Translate these snappy sentences into French.

- I always do the washing up.
- We have already visited France.
- Bertha was smoking heavily.
- Camping is good for your health.
- The children can speak English fluently.
- She soon became a fantastic film star.
- He only works one hour in the evening.

Answers on page 217.

Bigger and best, more or less

Believe it or not, comparing two things in French is blissfully straightforward (no, really!). You either put *plus* (more), *moins* (less) or *aussi* (as) in front of the adjective and *que* after it and *voilà*, you're done!

Naturally, you have to make sure that the spelling of the adjective agrees with the noun it describes, but that shouldn't cause you grief as you learnt/revised how to do that on page 43.

"Ma perruche est plus intelligente que ta mère."

"Ton père est moins intelligent que mon chien ..."

"...et ta sœur est aussi stupide que ton frère."

Mini word kit
une perruche . . . a budgerigar

There are, of course, some irregular forms . . . but given that there are only two of them, you can't really justify getting into a strop!

bon becomes *meilleur* (better)   *mauvais* becomes *pire* (worse)

> *Cette boum est **meilleure** que l'autre.*
> This party is **better** than the other one.

You can compare adverbs in the same way as adjectives.

> *Ma mamie rit **plus fort que** mon pépé.*
> My granny laughs **louder than** my grandad.

> *Mais personne ne rit **aussi fort que** toi!*
> But nobody laughs **as loudly as** you!

As before there are only two irregular forms to watch out for: *bien*, which becomes *mieux* (better) and *mal*, which becomes *pire* (worse).

> **Ce chien sent pire que l'autre.**
> This dog smells **worse** than the other one.

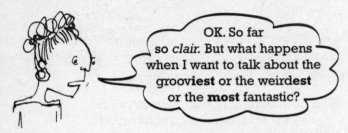

OK. So far so *clair*. But what happens when I want to talk about the **groovi**est or the weird**est** or the **most** fantastic?

Simple. You use either *le plus*, *la plus* or *les plus*.

> **Ma tante est la femme la plus gentille de Monte Carlo.**
> My aunt is **the kindest** woman in Monte Carlo.

> **Les plaisanteries de mon père sont les plus vieilles du monde.**
> My dad's jokes are **the oldest** in the world.

TOP TIP
If you want to say "the biggest", "best", etc. "<u>in</u>" . . . translate the "<u>in</u>" as *de*.

The same approach can be taken with *le moins*, *la moins* and *les moins*.

> **L'anglais est la matière la moins difficile pour eux.**
> English is their **least difficult** subject.

(Did you note how the spelling of the adjective always agrees with the noun it describes? If you didn't, note it now!)

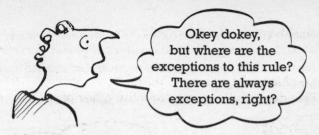

Bien sûr . . . but as before, the <u>only</u> words that don't play by the rules are *bon* and *mauvais*: *bon* changes to *le meilleur, la meilleure, les meilleurs* or *les meilleures* –

> **Hier, c'était *le meilleur* jour de ma vie.**
> Yesterday was **the best** day of my life.

– and *mauvais* changes to *le pire, la pire* or *les pires*.

Absolument! Check out these examples to see how it's done.

> *Mes parents parler, français **le moins couramment** de toute notre famille.*
> My parents speak French **the least fluently** of all our family.

> *Mon petit frère parle **le plus rapidement**.*
> My little brother speaks **the fastest**.

And what happens if I want to say "the best" or "the worst" plus a verb?

You simply put *le mieux* or *le pis* after the verb.

> *Pendant la Coupe du Monde, l'équipe française a joué **le mieux** et mon équipe a joué **le pis**.*
> During the World Cup, the French team played **the best** and my team played **the worst**.

PETIT TEST
1. Try your hand at translating these sentences into French.

- French cheeses are the best.
- You are singing better.
- I would like a better bike.
- Over there, it's worse.
- Have you something cheaper?
- Handball is less difficult than maths.

- I prefer rugby because it is more interesting than football.

2. How much do you know about France and the French? Answer this **true** or **false** quiz using complete sentences.

Exemple

Q. *La tour Eiffel est le batîment le plus haut de Paris. Vrai ou faux?*

A. *Vrai. La tour Eiffel est le batîment le plus haut de Paris.*

1. *L'Espagne est aussi grande que la France. Vrai ou faux?*
2. *Paris-ville est plus petit que Greater London. Vrai ou faux?*
3. *La religion la plus populaire de la France, c'est le catholicisme. Vrai ou faux?*
4. *Une baguette française mesure moins longue que 50 centimètres. Vrai ou faux?*
5. *La cité la plus grande de la France est Marseilles. Vrai ou faux?*
6. *La Loire n'est pas aussi longue que la Seine. Vrai ou faux?*
7. *"La Comédie Française" à Paris est le théâtre le plus célèbre de la France. Vrai ou faux?*
8. *Le français est parlé par plus de 200 millions de personnes du monde. Vrai ou faux?*

Answers on page 218.

Mini word kit

Paris-ville . . . the city of Paris

59

This, that, these, those

If by this stage in your study/revision programme you're in desperate need of small mercies, you'll be thrilled to learn/be reminded that the French words for "this", "that", "these" and "those" hold no surprises. Like other adjectives, they have masculine, feminine and plural spellings!

SINGULAR		**PLURAL**	
masculine	**feminine**	**masculine**	**feminine**
ce	*cette*	*ces*	*ces*
this/that	this/that	these/those	these/those

Cet is used before masculine singular nouns beginning with a vowel or **h**.

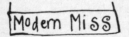

...et cette jupe ...
... and this skirt ...

Je voudrais ce sac à main ...
I would like this handbag ...

...et ces chaussures.
...and these shoes.

If you really want to emphasize something you are referring to, add **-ci** or **-là** after the noun.

Je voudrais aussi ce slip-là ...
I would also like that pair of knickers there ...

...et cet homme-ci ...
... and this man here ...

TOP TIP

If you want to say "I like it" or "I like that" or "I don't like it" or "I don't like that", use *ça*, e.g. *J'aime ça, je n'aime pas ça*. Unlike *ce* and *cette*, *ça* is often used when "that" doesn't refer to a named noun.

A word of warning: should you want to say "this one" or "that one", don't plonk an *un* or *une* after *ce* or *cette* and call it a day. Use one of these words instead:

SINGULAR		**PLURAL**	
masculine	**feminine**	**masculine**	**feminine**
celui	*celle*	*ceux*	*celles*
this one/that one		these ones/those ones	

Celui de Fred *est long mais* **ceux de Frank** *sont courts.*
Fred's one is long but **Frank's ones** are short.

Once again, if you want to make it really clear that what you are referring to is "this one" (here) or "that one" (there), add **-ci** or **-là** to *celui, celle, ceux* or *celles*.

Attendez!
Je voudrais
celui-ci, pas celui-là.
Wait! I'd like this
one, not that one.

Be possessive!

Have you got what it takes to be possessive in French? Find out by answering these three questions:

1. If you saw someone chatting up your boy/girlfriend in France, would you be able to say: "Oy, leave **my** boy/girlfriend alone."?

2. If a French motorist cut you up on the road and then blew a raspberry, would you have the vocab to shout: "And the same to you and **your** mother."?

3. If you and a mate met two French boys/girls you fancied on a camp site, would you know how to say: "Fancy a coffee back at **our** tent?"?

If you answered "No" to all of these questions, chances are you're not yet familiar with French possessives. These little words tell you <u>who</u> something belongs to, e.g. **my** girlfriend, **your** mother. The good news about French possessives is that they come before the noun just as they do in English. The bad news is that their spelling varies depending on the word that follows, e.g. *mon frère* – my brother (masculine singular) but *ma sœur* – my sister (feminine singular).

The following table shows all the possessives you could ever want to know. The easiest way to learn it is to chant it to yourself whenever and wherever you can, line by line, reading from left to right. Do this regularly and you'll soon discover that the words in it have rhythm, which helps make them easier to remember.

	Masc. sing.	Fem. sing.	Masc. and Fem. plural
My	mon	ma	mes
Your	ton	ta	tes

Continued…

	Masc. sing.	**Fem. sing.**	**Masc. and Fem. plural**
His/hers/its	son	sa	ses
Our	notre	notre	nos
Your	votre	votre	vos
Their	leur	leur	leurs

The author and publisher of this book take no responsibility for any damage done to your REPUTATION as a result of being caught chanting this table in public.

If a feminine singular noun begins with a vowel or **h**, use *mon, ton, son* instead of *ma, ta* and *sa*.

Now hold on *un instant.*
If *son, sa* and *ses* agree with the thing being possessed, how am I supposed to know whether they mean "his", "hers" or "its"?

You can usually tell what each word means from the context. Look at this example and you'll see for yourself:

> *Pierre a eu des vacances inoubliables. Je le sais parce qu'il m'a montré ses photos.*
> **Pierre has had an unforgettable holiday. I know because he showed me his photos.**

The French don't use **'s** when they want to talk about someone's belongings. So if you want to say something like "Simone's sausages" or "Eric's ears", use *de* or *des* instead.

Matt's motorbike.	*La moto de Matt.*
Esther's monkeys.	*Les singes d'Esther.*
The children's toy.	*Le jouet des enfants.*
The boys' boots.	*Les bottines des garçons.*

PETIT TEST

1. Have a go at translating these fascinating sentences into French!

- Next summer I am going to spend my holidays with my aunt.
- Yesterday evening Charlie went to a restaurant with his parents and his cousin, Bella.
- He always does his homework in their room.
- Our favourite subjects are English and art.
- Yesterday she went to the cinema because it was her best friend Jane's birthday.

2. Complete this cartoon conversation using these words: *ces, ce, celui-là, celle-ci, ce, cette, celui-ci, cette*

Answers on page 219.

The low-down on pronouns

Unless you have devised some ingenious way of sailing through your course and final exams without ever using a verb (and if you have, we'd all love to hear about it), you'll need to know how to use and recognize the French for "I", "you", "he", "she", "it", "we" and "they".

Just for the record, these words are known as subject pronouns, but <u>you</u> don't have to use this term, or any of the other grammatical terms in this book, if you don't want to.

je	I
tu	you
il/elle	he, she, it
on	one, we, they
nous	we
vous	you
ils/elles	they

(Remember, *je* becomes *j'* before a vowel, e.g. *j'ai* – I have)

The difference between *tu* and *vous* is straightforward. You use *tu* when you are talking to someone you know well or a child; and you use *vous* when you are talking to two or more people, or an adult who is not a relative or a close mate.

TOP TIP
Should you wish to be really condescending to someone in French (not advisable in your speaking exam!) opt for *tu* instead of the more formal *vous*. This will really make your words sting!

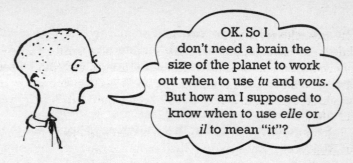

OK. So I don't need a brain the size of the planet to work out when to use *tu* and *vous*. But how am I supposed to know when to use *elle* or *il* to mean "it"?

Simple! *Elle* is used when "it" refers to a feminine noun and *il* is used when "it" refers to a masculine noun. The same rule more or less applies to *elles* and *ils*. *Elles* is used when all the things "they" refers to are feminine; and *ils* is used when one or more of the things "they" refers to is masculine . . . even if only one of those things is masculine.

So much for equality of the sexes, then!

J'ai un frère et douze sœurs. Ils ont tous de l'ail à la place d'un cerveau!
I have one brother and 12 sisters. They all have garlic for brains!

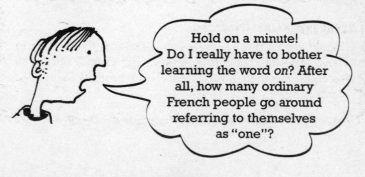

Hold on a minute! Do I really have to bother learning the word *on*? After all, how many ordinary French people go around referring to themselves as "one"?

You'd be amazed! It's true that in Britain only the Queen and posh people tend to use the word "one" to mean "we" or "they" (i.e. people in general), but in France, everyone uses *on* to mean "we" or "someone" or "they" (as in people in general).

> **On** *m'a dit que la reine dit "on" tout le temps.*
> **Someone** told me that the Queen says "one" all the time.

> *En France, on dit "on" tout le temps.*
> They (i.e. people) say "one" all the time in France.

Looking on the bright side, *on* uses the exact same form of verb as you would use with *il* or *elle* . . . so it's not as if you've got lots extra to learn!

(If you're a bit shaky when it comes to verb forms, see pages 7–27.)

Object pronouns: the facts!

me	me
te	you
le	him/it
la	her/it
nous	us
vous	you
les	them

In English, everyone, including the Queen, puts the words "me", "him", "her", "us" and "them" after the verb.

Can you see me?

The same applies to "you" and "it".*

Yes, I can see you.

In French, these words, known as object pronouns**, always go immediately <u>before</u> the verb, (not like in English).

*Tu **me** vois?*
*Oui, je **te** vois.*

If the verb is being used with an infinitive (i.e. the part of the verb that means "to . . ."), the object pronoun goes immediately <u>before</u> the infinitive.

verb   object   infinitive
(pronoun (

*Monsieur Rouge venait **nous** chercher à l'école.*
Mr Red was coming to collect **us** from school.

And if the verb is in the perfect tense (see page 16), the object pronoun goes before the *avoir* or *être*.

*Nous **l'**avons vu . . . et nous sommes sortis par la sortie de secours.*
We saw **him** . . . and left by the fire exit.

*Unless they are being used before the verb as subject pronouns – see page 70.
**Remember: there's no need for you to refer to these words as object pronouns if you don't want to. All that matters is that you recognize what they mean and use them properly.

When the last letter of a word and the first letter of the next are vowels, the first vowel is replaced by an apostrophe:

Tu m'entends, maman?
Can you hear me, mother?

Oui, je t'entends. Arrête de crier!
Yes, I can hear you. Stop shouting!

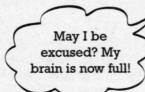

May I be excused? My brain is now full!

Object pronouns: more facts!

While we're still on the subject of object pronouns, it's worth swotting up on the following slightly different object pronouns, which also go in front of the verb.

me	to me
te	to you
lui	to him/ to her/ to it
nous	to us
vous	to you
leur	to them

*Tu **lui** passes le lait solaire?*
Can you pass **him** the suntan lotion?

Precise meaning: Can you pass the suntan lotion to him?

As you can see, unlike the French, we don't always bother to say "to". This means you must think carefully about the precise meaning of what you want to say when you are translating into French.

> *Je leur ai envoyé une lettre.*
> **I sent them a letter.**

Precise meaning: I sent a letter to them.

> *Ma mère m'a dit de laver la voiture.*
> **My mother told me to wash the car.**

Precise meaning: My mother said to me to wash the car.

Crystal clear? Jolly *bon*, because it's now time to find out/brush up on how to use several object pronouns together.

After you!

Using several object pronouns together in a sentence can seem like a bit of a palaver because if they are not placed in the correct order <u>in front</u> of the verb, the intended meaning of the sentence goes right out the window. Here's the order they should go in:

me	le	lui	y	en	
te	la	leur			} VERB
nous	les				
vous					

> *Je **le lui** ai donné ... et il **me l'**a rendu.*
> **I gave it to him ... and he gave it back to me.**

(For information about *y* and *en*, see page 159.)

PETIT TEST

Putting pronouns in the correct order without the help of a book takes practice, so start right now by translating the following sentences into French – be warned, they are arranged in order of difficulty. Once you've done that, read the following episode of the popular radio series, *More Tea, Vicar?*, and see if you can spot the deliberate mistake.

- Boy bands? I adore them!
- The headmistress wants to see us this afternoon.
- I offered him a new car.
- He gives it to me.
- The boys' letters? We will send them to them.
- The prizes? He presented them to us.

...and in today's episode of *More Tea, Vicar?* the vicar has some surprising news for Mrs A.

Madame A: *Monsieur le curé, vous dites que vous allez quitter notre village. Pourquoi est-ce que vous le quittez?*

Monsieur le curé: *Je le quitte parce qu'il est un trou.*

Madame A: *Et votre femme?*

Monsieur le curé: *Je l'ai vendue à mon voisin, Monsieur Bert.*

Madame A: *Vous lui l'avez vendue?*

Monsieur le curé: *Oui. Je la lui ai vendue hier soir.*

Silence

Madame A: *Encore une tasse de thé, Monsieur le curé?*

Answers on page 219.

Object pronouns: the saga continues!

Unbelievable though it may seem, there is a third (and final) set of object pronouns you need to be familiar with.

moi	I, me	*nous*	we, us
toi	you	*vous*	you
lui	he, him, it	*eux*	they, them
elle	she, her, it	*elles*	they, them
soi	himself, herself, itself, oneself, themselves		

These punchy little pronouns are used in several ways. . .

1. For emphasis:

> *Yann va passer l'aspirateur mais moi, je vais laver la voiture.*
> Yann is going to vacuum but I am going to wash the car.

> *Et toi, qu'est-ce que tu vas faire?*
> And you, what are you going to do?

77

2. In comparisons:

> *Mon lapin est plus intelligent que toi.*
> My rabbit is more intelligent than you.

3. After *c'est/c'était/ce sont*:

> *C'est moi! C'était lui!*
> It's me! It was him!

> *Ce sont elles!*
> It's them!

4. After prepositions:

> *chez lui; je compte sur eux; il pense souvent à elle.*
> at his house; I'm relying on them; he often thinks about her.

> (See page 79 for more about prepositions.)

5. After *ne . . . que*:

> *Il n'y a que moi.*
> There's only me.

> (See page 95 for more about *ne . . . que*.)

6. With *aussi*, *même* and *seul*:

> *Lui seul est capable de le faire.*
> Only he is capable of doing it.

7. In commands:

> *Passez-moi le sel, Trevor . . . donnez-le-moi!*
> Pass me the salt, Trevor . . . give it to me!

With, without, to and from!

Prepositions, i.e. words that describe where things are, such as "in", "on", "at", or when things happened, such as "before", "during" and "after", are really useful, so use them whenever you can. Below is a run-down of some common prepositions and their various uses. If the thought of working your way through yet another grammar section fills you with all the happiness of a heart condition, learn these prepositions (and the "But note" phrases) as part of your daily vocab fix. (See chapter 4, in particular page 109.)

à = to or at:

> *Je vais à Brighton. J'arriverai à minuit.*
> I am going **to** Brighton. I will arrive **at** midnight.

But note . . .
- *à gauche/à droite*   on the left/on the right
- *à mon avis*   in my opinion
- *à pied/à bicyclette/*   on foot/by bicycle/
  à moto/à cheval   by motorbike/on horseback
- *la fille aux cheveux bruns* the girl with brown hair

If you want to say "to the" . . . "at the" . . . etc., you must use *au* (*à + le*), *à la, à l'* or *aux* (*à+ les*).

masculine singular noun

Jacques se demandait s'il était allergique au potage.
Jacques was wondering if he was allergic **to the** soup.

feminine singular noun

*Neil a envoyé
ses parents à la lune.*
Neil has sent his parents
to the moon.

If the noun begins with **h**
or a vowel, use *à l'*:

A tout à l'heure.
See you soon.

noun plural

*Ce gendarme voudrait parler **aux** filles et **aux**
garçons de votre classe.*
This policeman would like to speak **to the** girls and
to the boys from your class.

noun plural

But note . . .

J'habite à Picardy	I live in Picardy (*à* + town or village = "in")
au Japon	to/in Japan (*au/aux* + masculine country = "to", "in")
aux Etats Unis	to/in the United States

de = of, from:

> *Le postiche **de** mon père vient de Londres.*
> My dad's toupée comes **from** London.

But note . . .

à six heures du matin (du soir)	at six in the morning (evening)
de cette façon	in this way, thus
de ce côté	on this side

Remember the words *du* (*de* + *le*), *de la, de l'* and *des* (*de* + *les*)? (See page 37 if you don't.) They also mean "of the", "from the":

> *Oliver a reçu un fax **de** son patron.*
> Oliver received a fax **from** his boss.

> *Son patron est **du** sud **de la** France.*
> His boss is **from** the south **of** France.

en = in:

> *En janvier, mon frère va à l'école **en** Italie. Il dit qu'il m'écrira **en** italien.*
> In January my brother is going to school **in** Italy. He says he'll write to me **in** Italian.

But note . . .

en voiture/en avion/en bus	by car/by plane/by bus
en bateau	by boat

en hiver/en automne/en été	in winter/autumn/summer
<u>but</u> *au printemps*	in spring
en ville <u>but</u> *à la campagne*	in town/in the country

TOP TIP

Always use *en* + feminine countries and languages, e.g. *en Angleterre* – in England, *en anglais* – in English. If you can't remember whether a country is masculine or feminine and you've no way of checking, use *en*. For some bizarre reason, most countries are feminine.

dans = in, into (often means "physically in" something):

Dans *cinq minutes, Madame X mettra ses enfants* **dans** *le placard et elle boira une tasse de thé.*
In five minutes' time, Madame X will put her children **in** the cupboard and have a cup of tea.

But note . . .
> *Il a pris un mouchoir de sa poche.*
> He took a hankerchief out of his pocket.

au dessus de = above, over the top of:

> *Ma chambre est **au dessus du** garage.*
> My bedroom is **over the** garage.

avant = before:

> *Je ne peux rien faire **avant** le déjeuner.*
> I can't do anything **before** lunch.

chez = at the house of, to the house of:

> *Allons **chez** moi!*
> Let's go to my **house!**

But note . . .
aller chez le médecin	to go to the doctor's
chez le boulanger	at the baker's

devant = before, in front of a place:

> *Ne gare jamais ta moto **devant** l'entrée d'une école.*
> Never park your motorbike **in front of** a school entrance.

entre = between, among:

> ***Entre** nous, ton voisin est un imbécile!*
> **Between** you and me, your neighbour is an idiot!

jusqu'à = as far as:

> *J'ai couru **jusqu'au** bout de la rue.*
> I ran **as far as the** end of the road.

par = by, through:

> *"J'en ai assez de cette leçon," a pensé Beryl, et elle a jeté son professeur **par** la fenêtre.*
> "I've had enough of this lesson," thought Beryl, and she threw her teacher **through** the window.

But note . . .

par terre	on the floor
trois fois par semaine	three times a week

pendant = during, for:

> *Qu'est-ce que tu as fait **pendant** la guerre, pépé?*
> What did you do **during** the war, grandpa?

But note . . .

> *J'ai travaillé pendant une heure et maintenant, je veux me reposer.*
> I have worked for one hour and now I want to have a rest.

pour = in order to, for (as in pre-arranged time limit):

> *Allô maman. Je téléphone **pour** dire que je serai en retenue pour deux semaines.*
> Hello Mum. I'm phoning **to** say that I will be in detention for two weeks.

près de = by, next to:

> *Assieds-toi **près de** moi, jeune homme!*
> Sit **by** me, young man!

But note . . .

> *Ma grand-mère a près de quatre-vingt ans.*
> My grandmother is nearly 80.

sans = without:

> *Mon Dieu! Le curé est parti **sans** sa gaine!*
> Good heavens! The vicar has left **without** his girdle!

sous = under:

> *Ton pantalon est*
> ***sous** le lit, papa.*
> **Your trousers**
> **are under the**
> **bed, dad.**

sur = on, upon:

> *Vos bottines sont*
> ***sur** la table.*
> **Your boots are**
> **on the table.**

But note . . .
> *Neuf élèves sur dix disent qu'ils détestent le français!*
> Nine out of ten pupils say they hate French!

vers = towards:

> *. . . et il s'est tourné **vers** moi et il a dit . . .*
> . . . and he turned **to** me and said . . .

But note . . .
> *Henri va arriver vers six heures.*
> Henri is going to arrive at about six o'clock.

PETIT TEST

Imagine this. You get back from college one day only to find that your mum has braved the plague pit that is your room and tidied it up. In the process she has removed your most precious possessions from their usual resting place and put them elsewhere. Check through your list of possessions below and then jot down where they can now be found.

Answers on page 220.

- *Une photo de Keith Chegwin.*
  La photo de Keith Chegwin est devant l'ordinateur.

- *Une paire de baskets.*
- *Un jean en cuir.*
- *Des CDs.*
- *Un téléphone.*
- *Des magasins du football.*
- *Un journal.*
- *Une vidéocassette de Keith Chegwin.*

Make the link!

If you want to speak and write French with anything remotely resembling pace and style, you'll need to have a few words up your sleeve that will provide links between your sentences. Here are a few you'd do well to be familiar with!

Link word	Translation	Word-doctor's orders
alors	so, for that reason	only to be used in the middle of a sentence
car	because, as	
comme	as	
depuis que	since	only to be used in expressions of time
dès que	as soon as	
donc	therefore, so	only to be used in the middle of a sentence
et	and	
lorsque	when	
ou	or	
mais	but	
parce que	because	
pendant que	while, whilst	use only when referring to time
puisque	since	only use when "since" could mean "because"
si	if	

> *D'habitude, je fais mes devoirs **mais** hier soir,*
> *je suis allé(e) à la pêche.*
> Usually I do my homework **but** yesterday evening
> I went fishing.
>
> *Pour aller à l'école, je mets une jupe longue **et** une*
> *veste, **ou** un pantalon et un tee-shirt.*
> For school I wear a long skirt **and** a jacket, **or** a
> pair of trousers and a T-shirt.

Who the heck are you?

> ### The who's who word kit
>
> *qui* = who, which, that   *que* = who, whom, that
> *à qui* = to whom   *où* = where, in which
> *dont* = whose, of whom,
>   of which

Using *qui* when you should have used *que* is like watching telly
when you should be studying, i.e. it's a bad habit that's hard to
break! Working out when to use each of these words isn't
fiendishly difficult though, provided you remember the following
important difference:

Qui is usually followed immediately by the verb, while *que* is
usually separated from the verb by a noun or pronoun, e.g.

verb

*La femme **qui** habite avec Pierre est une actrice.*
The woman **who** lives with Pierre is an actress.

pronoun verb

*Le train **que** nous avons pris est tombé en panne.*
The train (**that**) we took broke down.

In English we don't always bother to add "that", "which", "of which", "of whom", etc., whereas the French always do. This means you must think very carefully about the precise meaning of what you want to say when you are translating into French.

Here's the bottle of beer I bought.
*Voici la bouteille de bière **que** j'ai achetée.**

*When you use **que** with the perfect or pluperfect tense, the past participle usually agrees with the preceding direct object. If you've got no idea what the heck a past participle or direct object are, see page 20. If you've got no idea what the perfect tense is, see page 16. And if you've got no idea what **que** means . . . you haven't been concentrating for some time, have you?

Question time!

If you want to interrogate someone in French, you can either . . .

a) Raise the tone of your voice at the end of a statement, e.g.

Tu es un imbécile?
Are you an idiot?

(This is fine in conversation; not so brilliant if you are writing!)

or

b) Add *est-ce que* to the beginning of a statement, e.g.

Est-ce que tu es un imbécile?
Are you an idiot?

or

c) Add *n'est-ce pas* to the end of a statement. This is like adding "isn't it?", "doesn't he?", "haven't we?", "can't she?", etc., e.g.

> *Tu es un imbécile, n'est-ce pas?*
> **You're an idiot, aren't you?**

or

d) Swap the order of the verb and the subject, e.g.

> *Es-tu un imbécile?*
> **Are you an idiot?**

TOP TIP
If the *il/elle/on* form of a verb ends in *-e* or *-a*, add a *-t* before the *il/elle/on* if swapping the order of the verb and subject. This will make your question easier to pronounce.

> *Joue-t-il aujourd'hui?*
> **Is he playing today?**

The essential interrogator's word kit

quand	when?
combien de	how much, how many?
comment	how?
pourquoi	why?
où	where?
d'où	from where?
qu'est-ce que	what?
qui	who? whom?
à quelle heure	at what time?

Comment *ça va?*
How are you?

Tu fais **combien de** *devoirs le soir?*
How much homework do you do in the evening?

Où *habites-tu?*
Where do you live?

Qu'est-ce que *tu as fait pendant les vacances?*
What did you do during the holidays?

Qui *a pris mon anorak?*
Who has taken my anorak?

Vous êtes allé au cinéma avec **qui**?
Who did you go to the cinema with?

PETIT TEST

Have you got what it takes to be a French interrogator?
Knowing the French words for "when" and "where" is one
thing, but knowing how to use them correctly is another
kettle of crayons entirely. To find out whether you've got
what it takes to be an effective French interrogator, try this
mini quiz.

1. You wake up one morning in 1791 to find two French
aristocrats at your door in search of asylum from the
French revolution.

"*Quand est-ce que vous avez quitté la France?*" you ask.
"*Je quitte la France hier soir,*" replies the first aristocrat.
"*Et j'ai quitté la France hier matin,*" replies the other.
"*Attendez un instant!*" you cry. "One of you aristos isn't
a Frenchie at all!"
Which one do you suspect and why?

2. It's 1940 and you are a British agent working
undercover in German-occupied France. In a café, you
spot a woman who you think may be an undercover
agent like yourself. To check if your suspicions are
correct, you ask her the following questions:

Comment vous appelez-vous?   *Je m'appelle Fifi Fou-Fou.*
D'où venez vous, Fifi Fou-Fou? *Je viens de Paris.*
Faites vous habiter à Paris?   *Oui. Je fais habiter à Paris.*

Which of your questions is the trick one?
Is Fifi Fou-Fou a fellow agent or not?

Answers on page 220.

Be positive about negatives!

Being negative in English is easy (particularly first thing on a Monday morning) because most English negatives are made up of one word:

Nobody looks good in dungarees.
Nothing ever happens in Eastbourne.
Nudist barbecues are **never** a good idea.

In French, however, most negatives are made up of two parts:

Negative word kit

ne . . . pas	not
ne . . . jamais	never
ne . . . rien	nothing
ne . . . plus	no longer, no more
ne . . . point	not at all
ne . . . personne	no one
ne . . . que	only
ne . . . ni . . . ni . . .	neither . . . nor

Generally speaking, these two parts go either side of the verb when it is in the present tense . . .

Sans le foot, la vie n'est pas amusante.
Without football, life is not fun.

. . . and on either side of the *avoir* or *être* when the verb is in the perfect or pluperfect tense:

L'année dernière, mon père a passé par la douane en transportant une noix de coco dans son caleçon. On n'a jamais osé le fouiller.

Last year, my dad went through customs carrying a coconut in his underpants. They **never** dared search him.

If there is a pronoun before the verb, that too is usually sandwiched between the negatives:

> *Le douanier m'a demandé pourquoi mon père se promenait comme un cow-boy, mais je **ne** lui ai **rien** dit.*
> The customs officer asked me why my father was walking like a cowboy, but I told him **nothing**.

If there is an infinitive in the sentence, both parts of the negative come before the infinitive:

> *J'ai décidé de **ne plus** voyager avec mon père.*
> I have decided to travel with my father **no longer**.

Step-by-step guide to being negative

If you have trouble translating into French sentences with pronouns and a negative in them, such as "I didn't see him" or "He didn't give it to her", follow this four-point plan and see if it helps.

1. Change the verb in English from the negative to the positive, e.g. "I didn't see" becomes "I did see" or "I saw".

2. Write out the positive version of the verb in French, e.g. *J'ai vu* – "I saw".

3. Put the pronoun in place, e.g. *Je l'ai vu* – "I saw him".

4. Then sandwich the pronoun and the verb, or the pronoun and the *avoir/être* part of the verb, between the negatives, e.g. *Je ne l'ai pas vu* – "I didn't see him".

To translate a negative sentence without a pronoun into French, simply miss out step **3**.

Secret thoughts of the examiner
We examiners are a perverse lot who love to see irregular gramatical forms used correctly. So if you've got your sights set on getting a Grade A in your final exams, try to use these two important negatives that don't play by the rules: *ne . . . personne* and *ne . . . que*.

In tenses that use *avoir/être* and a past participle, the *personne* part of *ne . . . personne* goes <u>after</u> the past participle, e.g.

> **Tu n'as vu personne?**
> **Didn't you see anyone?**

And the *que* in *ne . . . que* always goes in front of whichever word "only" applies to, e.g.

> **Il n'est comme cela que le dimanche.**
> **He is like that only on Sundays.**

TOP TIP
A great grade-grabbing phrase you could use in your writing or speaking is *je n'oublierai jamais* – "I will never forget . . ."

Je n'oublierai jamais cette semaine/ce film/ces vacances avec ton porc-épic.
I'll never forget that week/that film/that holiday with your porcupine.

PETIT TEST

Translate these sentences into French and find out how much you can remember about . . .

. . . linking words:

- I like my best friend a lot because he's funny.
- I like to sunbathe when the weather's fine.
- We went into a café where we ate a delicious meal.

. . . *qui* and *que*:

- My bedroom is big with a window that overlooks the road.
- I went to see my aunt who was living nearby.
- Yesterday I had an accident that was quite serious.

. . . and negatives:

- I don't like that!
- She didn't go into town this evening.
- I will never forget that party.
- Tomorrow I'm going to do nothing!

Answers on page 220.

Dictionaries drive me demented!

If there were a prize for the most underrated book on the planet, the French/English dictionary would be a strong contender, alongside David Beckham's Wonderful Things To Do With Pastry.

Your French/English dictionary is indispensable when it comes to doing course work and stuff. If you use yours properly, your grades should improve dramatically. If you use it badly, your grades will sink like a stone. In fact, many of the major clangers made in French GCSE are committed by students who have misused their dictionaries. For example, there was once a student who wished to write "I want to explore the bottom of the sea" in French. As she didn't know the French for "bottom", she turned to her bilingual dictionary. However, instead of looking through all the entries for "bottom" to find the correct one for her sentence, she picked the first word that caught her eye, in this case *derrière*. Unfortunately, the noun *derrière* means "bottom" as in "buttocks", so her finished sentence translated as:

I want to explore the buttocks of the sea.

No wonder teachers often need a stiff drink at the end of the day!

Dictionary rules OK

Like most things in life, your bilingual dictionary will only be of value to you if you know how to use it properly. If you're not sure how to do just that, here are some golden rules you may find helpful:

1. Make sure you understand what your dictionary's main abbreviations mean, e.g. **n** after a word means the word is a noun; **nm** means it's a masculine noun; **nf** means it's a feminine noun; **a** means the word's an adjective; **adv** means it's an adverb, etc. (If you don't know the difference between a noun, adjective, adverb, etc., turn to chapter 2.) There should be a list of all the abbreviations and their meanings at the front of your dictionary.

2. When you look up a word, make sure you find the right translation. For example, if you are looking up the word for "park", as in a place with swings and dog mess, be sure to find the noun *un parc* rather than the verb *garer*, which means "to park a car". To ensure you've got the right type of word, <u>always</u> check it in the other half of your dictionary. This may sound a drag, but it will improve your French vocab in the long run.

3. If you are looking up a word that has more than one meaning, make sure you check all the meanings given to find the one you had in mind, otherwise you too may find yourself exploring the sea's "buttocks" instead of its "bottom".

4. When looking up a verb, remember that the dictionary will give you the verb in its infinitive, or neutral, form, i.e. *presser* – "to squeeze". It's down to you to change the infinitive into the form you need, e.g. *je presse* – "I squeeze".

100

pronunciation
guide

This tells you that the word given
means "to squeeze" as in "to press"

squeeze (skwiz) vt (press) presser;

abbreviation for verb   infinitive

> **TOP TIP**
> Don't be alarmed by the different abbreviations given for
> verbs in your dictionary, e.g. **vt** – transitive verbs; **vi** –
> intransitive verbs. So long as you recognize that these
> different abbreviations all refer to verbs, you'll be OK.

5. Remember! If you don't learn how French works and how the
words fit together, your dictionary won't be a lot of use to you.
This is partly because word-for-word translation rarely works.
For example, if you want to say: "I hate French. I want to give
it up", you can't just look up each of these words in turn and
write down the first translation you find. If you did, you'd
probably end up with:

Je détester français. Je vouloir donner il là-haut.

This is the French equivalent of double Dutch. Instead, you
have to think about the structure of what you are trying to say.
For example, ask yourself: might there be a French verb that
specifically means "to give up"? Once you've sussed out the
structure of the sentence, you then have to change the words
you find in the dictionary into their correct form, e.g.

Je déteste le français. Je veux l'abandonner.

6. Looking up the words you need in your dictionary will become quicker and easier with practice . . . but nothing beats learning those words, and how they work, by heart!

Odd endings

One of the really great things about your French/English dictionary is it can remind you of all those grammatical irregularities that you think were invented solely to give you grief, such as unusual plurals and weird feminine forms of adjectives. Often only the endings of feminine and plural forms are given to save space, so make sure you check out the mock dictionary page below to see how this type of information is put across. The smartest thing to do when you discover irregular forms is to take a deep breath and learn them. That way they won't be able to panic you when they crop up in your final exams.

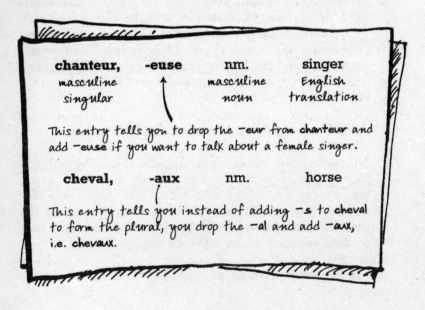

chanteur,　　**-euse**　　**nm.**　　**singer**
masculine　　　　　　masculine　　English
singular　　　　　　noun　　　　translation

This entry tells you to drop the -eur from chanteur and add -euse if you want to talk about a female singer.

cheval,　　**-aux**　　**nm.**　　**horse**

This entry tells you instead of adding -s to cheval to form the plural, you drop the -al and add -aux, i.e. chevaux.

                 plural   adjective

beau,   **belle,**   pl. **beaux,** **belles** a. beautiful

masculine feminine   masculine feminine   translation

singular   singular   plural

feminine singular made   No entry given for feminine
by dropping the −al and   plural so it must follow
adding −ale, e.g. égale.   normal rules, i.e. égales.

                             adjective

égal,   **-ale,** **-aux**   (egal)   a.   equal

masculine   pronunciation   translation

singular   guide

masculine plural made by dropping −al from égal and
adding −aux, e.g. égaux.

TOP TIP

Take care not to get caught out by the adjectives *beau* (beautiful), *nouveau* (new) and *vieux* (old). When used in front of a masculine singular noun that begins with a vowel or **h**, they change to *bel* (beautiful), *nouvel* (new) or *vieil* (old).

Another way in which your dictionary saves space is to list variations of a word without writing that word out in full each time. For example, if you were to look up "book" in the English/French part of your dictionary, you might find within that entry the French for **to b. up** meaning "to book up", **to b. in** meaning "to check into a hotel" and **-ing** meaning "booking".

PETIT TEST

If you haven't given your French/English dictionary much attention in a long time, here's a quick exercise to help you break down the barriers. The bracketed words in the following police report don't make their plurals by simply adding -s. Use your dictionary to discover how unusual their plural forms really are.

(Madame) et (monsieur), il y a un voleur dans notre village! Hier il a volé des (bijou) et des (chou) aux deux (château) sur la colline et aujourd'hui il a volé les (feu) devant les (bureau) de (mademoiselle) Collette et Claire. Je vous supplie de garder les (œil) ouverts et de chercher ce voleur. Si vous le voyez, signalez ce fait à la police.

If you need a translation or want to check your answers, turn to page 221.

Your dictionary and the exam

Chances are you won't be allowed to use your dictionary in your final GCSE exams, so unless you want to find yourself stranded up a certain creek without a paddle, it's important that you familiarize yourself with the French words and phrases most often used in exam questions. Even if it turns out that you are allowed to use your dictionary in the exams (if in doubt, check with your teacher) it's still important that you can translate exam questions unaided because looking up question words and phrases during an exam is a waste of valuable time. So, wherever you stand *vis-a-vis* dictionaries and the exams, do yourself a favour and learn to recognize the words and phrases below:

voici un exemple
here is an example

à votre avis
in your opinion

en chiffres
in numbers

donnez les détails suivants
give the following details

choisissez la description qui correspond le mieux . . .
choose the description which best fits . . .

complétez la table
complete the table

répondez en français ou cochez les cases
answer in French or tick the boxes

vrai
true

faux
false

d'abord
first

dessinez
draw

elle écrit au sujet de
she is writing about

en anglais
in English

lisez les questions/la liste, etc.
read the questions/the list, etc.

écrivez le numéro, etc.
write the number, etc.

les réponses suivantes
the following answers

répondez aux questions
answer the questions

trouvez les phrases
find the sentences

lisez attentivement
read carefully

remplissez les blancs
fill in the blanks

corrigez l'affirmation
correct the statement

indiquez
show, indicate

faites correspondre
match up

regardez les dessins/la grille, etc.
look at the drawings/
the grid, etc.

cochez les cases appropriées
tick the appropriate boxes

écoutez attentivement
listen carefully

notez
note

mettez
put

encerclez
circle

Don't forget question words such as *quand, comment,* etc.
(See page 93.)

Spell check!

One final point about using your French/English dictionary: when you use the English/French side of it, make sure you look up the <u>correct</u> spelling of the English word. OK, so this sounds obvious, but you'd be amazed at the number of gaffes made by students who have looked up the wrong spelling of a word. For example, one ex-student, who wanted to write about his tedious neighbour, looked up the word "boar" (as in pig-like animal) instead of "bore" (as in boring person). His disturbing essay about the boar next door is still discussed in staff rooms today!

107

What's the French for how the heck am I supposed to learn all this vocab?

When asked whether they'd prefer to shoot themselves in the foot or learn French vocab, a percentage of GCSE students remained undecided.

If you've been flicking through the complete list of set vocab in your syllabus and are now in the process of dialling the Samaritans, hang up. Yes, it's true, you are expected to know a lot of words to get through your course and exam, but no, the number isn't limitless and with any luck you're familiar with some of these words already. Besides, there are plenty of foolproof dos and don'ts when it comes to learning GCSE French vocab, as you are about to discover.

Vocab-learning dos and vocab-learning don'ts

Don't . . . leave vocab learning to the last minute. Start well in advance of your final exams and spend about ten minutes every day (and that includes today) learning new words. Learning a little *often* is a heck of a lot easier than learning lots at once.

Do . . . be canny and think about which words you are likely to need in your written or spoken work, and which you are only likely to come across while reading or listening. The former you'll need to learn properly – and that includes learning their gender, spelling and pronunciation – but with the latter, you really only need know what they look and sound like and what they mean.

Don't . . . kid yourself you can learn vocab while watching TV, listening to the radio or cooking a meal, etc. You can't. If you could, you would have been bilingual long ago!

Do . . . work through the vocab for all the topics in your syllabus and concentrate on a different one each day. It's better to be familiar with vocab from all topics than to know just a few inside out. (If you've forgotten or don't know what these topics are, see page 113.)

Don't . . . forget the tips for learning genders given on page 36.

Do . . . scribble down each word or phrase you learn a couple of times to improve your spelling, and repeat the words out loud too. You're much less likely to drift off into a daydream if you make yourself write out the words as you learn them.

Don't . . . invite a mate round to test you unless you're both determined not to gossip. Revising with a mate is all very well, but unless you write down each word, your spelling won't improve.

Do . . . make up a sentence for each word you learn. This sounds a chore, it's true, but it really will help you master French spelling and grammar a lot more quickly. Remember to check your sentence with your coursebook/teacher/French language assistant to see whether you got it right.

Don't . . . fall for the old trick of playing a tape of French vocab while you sleep in the hope it will turn you into Emmanuel Petit or Vanessa Paradis. The words may seep into your subconscious during the night, but there's no guarantee they'll reappear when you want them.

Do . . . begin each vocab-learning session with a written test on what you learnt the day before and then check your answers. If writing isn't possible – perhaps because there's a sudden world shortage of pens – test yourself by covering first the English list of words, then the French list.

Don't . . . bone up on French slang taught to you by your mates unless you've checked it out first. There's nothing worse than saying something horribly offensive without even realizing it.

Do . . . check the gender and spelling of words you think you already know. You'd be amazed how easy it is to convince yourself you know how to spell a word correctly when you don't.

TOP TIP

Write your French vocabulary on plain postcards or Post-It notes and stick them around the house – on your mirror, beside the loo, above your bed, etc. That way you can take in snippets of vocab when otherwise you might just be staring into space.

même(s) same

Nous avons le
même anniversaire.
We have the same
birthday.

autre(s) other

Mon autre frigo
est un congélateur.
My other fridge is
a freezer.

chaque
each (always singular)

chaque homme,
chaque femme.
Each man, each woman.

plusieurs
several (always plural)

J'ai plusieurs
copines.
I have several
girlfriends.

tout (m.s.), toute (f.s.),
tous (m. pl.),
toutes (f. pl.)
all, every

J'aime toute ma famille!
I love all my family!
(P.S. Dad can you lend
me £500?)

quelque(s)   some

J'ai acheté
quelques CDs.
I bought some CDs.

n'importe qui   anyone

N'importe qui peut
parler le français!
Anyone can speak French!

n'importe quoi   anything

Mon frère mange
n'importe quoi.
My brother eats anything.

quelqu'un   someone

Il y a quelqu'un
dans ce placard.
There's someone in
this cupboard.

quelque chose
something

J'attends quelque
chose.
I am waiting
for something.

chacun(e)   each one

Chacune de ces filles.
Each one of these girls.

Topic tester

All the vocab you are expected to be familiar with for your course and final exams is arranged in topics and can be found in your coursebook/s and/or in the lists given to you by your teacher. You can even buy books with GCSE vocabulary in them too. Next you'll find a run-down of your GCSE topics. For each one, jot down nine words in French that relate to that topic and then write out a sentence that includes at least one of your nine words. (The word and sentence printed under each topic title are examples only, so don't cheat and use them as part of your answers!) If you can't come up with enough words or a sentence from memory, use your coursebook/vocab lists to help you. When you're done, check your spelling and grammar, then read your lists out loud to practise your pronunciation. If you think you might not have to learn vocabulary from all of these topics for your final exam, check with your teacher.

Language of the classroom
une question   a question

> *Je suis desolé(e) mais je n'ai pas compris la question.*
> **I'm sorry but I didn't understand the question.**

School
une matière   a subject

> *Ma matière préférée, c'est le français.*
> **My favourite subject is French.**

Home life
un appartement   a flat

> *J'habite un grand appartement au sud de Sheffield.*
> I live in a big flat south of Sheffield.

Media
une pièce de théâtre   a play

> *Hier soir, j'ai vu une bonne pièce de théâtre.*
> I saw a good play last night.

Health and fitness
la gorge   the throat

> *J'ai mal à la gorge.*
> I've got a sore throat.

Food and drink
un café-crème   a white coffee

> *Je prends un sandwich au fromage et un café-crème.*
> I'll have a cheese sandwich and a white coffee.

You, family and friends
une belle-mère   a step-mother

> *Mon père est au chômage et ma belle-mère travaille dans un bureau.*

My dad is out of work and my step-mother works in an office.

Free time, holidays and special occasions

une semaine   a week

> *La semaine dernière je suis allé(e) en ville et j'ai acheté des vêtements.*
> Last week I went to town and bought some clothes.

Personal relationships and social activities

s'amuser   to have fun

> *Je me suis très bien amusé(e).*
> I had lots of fun.

Arranging a meeting or activity

après-demain   the day after tomorrow

> *Après-demain on va au match.*
> We're going to the match the day after tomorrow.

Leisure and entertainment

un film d'épouvante   a horror film

> *A mon avis, ce film d'épouvante était nul.*
> In my opinion that horror film was rubbish.

Home town, local environment and customs

la campagne the countryside

> *J'habite une ville industrielle dans le sud-ouest du Pays de Galles mais je préférerais habiter la campagne.*
> I live in an industrial town in the south west of Wales but I would prefer to live in the country.

Finding the way

un office de tourisme a tourist office

> *Pour aller à l'office de tourisme, s'il vous plaît?*
> How do I get to the tourist office please?

Shopping

acheter to buy

> *Où est-ce que je pourrais acheter des baskets?*
> Where can I buy some trainers?

Public services

un téléphone a telephone

> *Où est le téléphone public le plus près d'ici?*
> Where's the nearest public telephone from here?

Getting around

un car a coach

Le car pour Paris part à quelle heure?
What time does the coach for Paris leave?

Further education and training

l'université   university

Après l'école je voudrais faire des études à l'université
After school I would like to go to university.

Careers and employment

un bureau   an office

Je travaille dans un bureau seulement le mercredi.
I work in an office only on Wednesdays.

Advertising and publicity

les renseignements   information

Avez-vous des renseignements du syndicat d'initiative?
Have you any information from the tourist information office?

Communication

allô   hello

Allô. Puis-je parler à Monsieur Brun?
Hello. Can I speak to Mr Brown?

Life in other countries/communities

une livre sterling   a pound sterling

> *Je veux changer dix livres sterling.*
> I want to change £10.

Tourism

les vacances   the holidays

> *Pendant les vacances je suis allé(e) en Grèce en avion.*
> During the holidays I went to Greece by plane.

Accommodation

une chambre avec   a double room
un grand lit

> *Je voudrais réserver une chambre avec un grand lit pour la nuit du seize mars.*
> I'd like to reserve a double room for the night of March 16.

The wider world

espagnol   Spanish

> *Mon ami est espagnol.*
> My friend is Spanish.

Read any good French lately?

5

Selon une étude récente plus de neuf jeunes français sur dix peuvent comprendre cette phrase.

You don't need a book to tell you the more French you read, the better. So do yourself a favour and read as wide a variety of French texts as you can and make a point of learning the words you don't know. If the only French book you have at home is your coursebook, try and get hold of easy books in French aimed at kids and French newspapers and magazines. There are also some great magazines on the market designed specifically for GCSE French students such as *Ça Va* and *Chez Nous* that you could look at. (Telephone Mary Glasgow Magazines on (01926) 815560 if you want to take out a subscription.)

If you're not wild about reading books and magazines in French because you fear you'll end up looking up so many words you'll soon lose the plot, don't despair. For a start, it's highly unlikely you'll need to understand every single word to follow the gist of the text. Provided you look up any words you absolutely need to know to make sense of the text, you should be able to guess the meaning of some of the rest by looking at them in context and by using your knowledge of French grammar.

OH YEAH?

No, really! After all, just think how many times you've come across a word you don't know in an English novel or newspaper article and rather than lose the thread of what you're reading by looking it up, you've used your knowledge of English grammar and the rest of the sentence or paragraph to help you guess its meaning. For example, let's say you came across this sentence and didn't know what the word "uncharitably" means:

**"She's got all the compassion of a rock cake,"
said Millie uncharitably.**

You could probably guess the meaning of "uncharitably" by looking at how it is put together. For a start, you know that **-ly** at the end of a word often means it's an adverb (e.g. "quickly", "slowly") so you know "uncharitably" explains <u>how</u> Millie says what she says. You also know that **un-** at the start of a word often means "not" (e.g. "unknown" = not known). Therefore "uncharitably" could mean <u>not + charitable + ly</u>. If you then know, or can guess, what the word "charity" means, you should be able to work out what "uncharitably" means.

Like the English language, French has certain patterns that, once you get to know them, can give you a big clue as to what unknown words mean. For example:

- The letters **mi-** in front of a word mean "half", e.g. *mi-temps*, half-time; *à mi-temps*, part-time; *mi-mars*, mid-March.

  *Madame Smith était **à mi-chemin** quand elle s'est rendue compte qu'elle avait laissé son bébé dans le bus.*
  Mrs Smith was **halfway along the road** when she realized she'd left her baby on the bus.

120

- The letters **in-** or **im-** added on to the front of a word often mean "not" + "something", e.g. *inconnu*, not known, unknown.

Which of these words
best describes you?
utile	useful
populaire	popular
conscient	conscious
inutile	useless
inconscient	unconscious
impopulaire	unpopular

- As in English, the letters **re-** or **ré-** in front of a word often mean "again", e.g. *recommencer*, to start again.

Kevin s'apprêtait à refaire son examen de français.
Kevin was getting ready to re-take his French exam.

- **Sous-** in front of a word often means "under" or "underneath", eg. *sous-marine*, underwater; *sous-titres*, subtitles.

The final letters of a word can give you a clue to its meaning too. For example:

- Words that end in **-ment** often end in **-ly** in English, e.g. *complètement*, completely; *rarement*, rarely; *brièvement*, briefly. (See pages 49–50 for more about words ending in **-ment.**)

- The letters **-ette** added to the end of a word often make the word mean something smaller, e.g. *la fille* – the girl, but *la fillette* – the little girl.

- Nouns that end in **-é**, **-e** or **-ée** in French often end in **-y** in English, e.g. *charité*, charity; *pureté*, purity; *l'identité*, identity.

- The ending **-eur** or **-euse** tells you the word refers to a type of person, e.g. *chanter*, to sing; *chanteur*, a male singer; *chanteuse*, a female singer.

- The letters **-ier** and **-ière** at the end of a word can tell you whether the person is a man or woman, e.g. *infirmier*, male nurse; *infirmière*, female nurse.

● The word **-aine** added to a number means "about".

> *La chaîne hi-fi de mon père a une centaine d'ans.*
> **My dad's hi-fi is about 100 years old.**

These spelling rules may also help you work out what an unfamiliar word means.

● As in English, words that end in **-able** often have the meaning "able to be", e.g. *mangeable*, edible (i.e. *manger* (to eat) + **-able** (able to be)).

> *Je vous remercie pour cette course inoubliable.*
> **Thank you for the unforgettable ride.**

● The ending **-que** is often **-ic** in English, e.g. *le plastique*, plastic; *nostalgique*, nostalgic.

- The symbol **^** over a letter can show that there would be an **s** in English, e.g. *coûter*, to cost; *intérêt*, interest.

Un homme et un poulet rôti se sont installés dans la Nouvelle Forêt. Les voisins disent que c'est dégoûtant!
Man and roast chicken set up home in the New Forest. Neighbours say it's disgusting!

- When a French word ends in **-ant**, the English equivalent usually ends in **-ing**, e.g. v*enant*, coming; *allant*, going; *arrivant*, arriving; *disant*, saying.

EXTRA! EXTRA!
Verbs ending in **-ant** are called present participles. To form the present participle of a verb, take the *nous* form of the present tense, drop the **-ons**, add **-ant** and you're done! The only exceptions (aaarggh!) are *être*, which becomes *étant*; *avoir*, which becomes *ayant*; and *savoir*, which becomes *sachant*.

TOP TIP

Remember, one of the best ways to improve your GCSE reading is to learn your set vocab and make sure that you can tell the difference between different verb tenses. See page 113 if you want reminding of the set vocabulary topics. Check with your teacher if you think you might not have to learn vocabulary from the full range of topics.

False French

Now as you probably know, there are many words in French that are spelt in a similar, if not the same, way as in English, e.g. *le gouvernement* – the government; *le nombre* – the number; *le sandwich* – the sandwich! This is, of course, fabulous news, as the similarities can often help you guess what an unfamiliar French word means. HOWEVER . . . wait for it . . . there are also a few common French words that look like English words but in fact, have wildly different meanings!

Dear Lord, please let this be a wind-up.

125

If that's what you're thinking, open your French/English dictionary and see for yourself how many of the following words don't mean what you'd think they mean!

assister à:	le médecin: ....
les cabinets:	la monnaie: ....
le car:	passer: ....
car:	le photographe: ....
causer:	la place: ....
la cave:	le plat: ....
la pièce:	rester: ....
la journée:	sensible: ....
la lecture:	la veste: ....
farter:	les baskets: ....

PETIT TEST

Your pen pal's mum asks you to take "*la Métro*" into the centre of Paris to pick up some groceries for supper. Do you . . .

a) drive her old Mini Metro car to the centre and pick up some tasty snacks?

b) take the underground to the centre and pick up some tasty snacks?

c) stay where you are and order a takeaway?

Answer on page 221.

126

Which spotting!

Remember those three little words *qui*, *que* and *dont*? (See page 90 if you don't.) Well, the following variations of these words have a habit of cropping up in GCSE reading texts, so it's worth getting used to what they look like!

ce qui	which/what
ce que	which/what
ce dont	which/what

Here's a selection of other words you may come across, all of which mean "which".

lequel (m.s.)	*auquel*	*duquel*
laquelle (f.s.)	*à laquelle*	*de laquelle*
lesquels (m.pl.)	*auxquels*	*desquels*
lesquelles (f. pl.)	*auxquelles*	*desquelles*

So, no chance of the word "which" dropping out of the French language then!

Secret thoughts of the examiner

Using *ce qui*, *lequel*, *auquel*, *duquel*, etc. in your writing or speaking will really make my day! So if you think you can handle it, get your head around the following:

- *ce qui* is used when "which/what" is the subject of the next verb, e.g.

  Dites-moi ce qui se passe.
  Tell me what's happening.

- *ce que* is used when "which/what" is the object of the next verb (that means there's usually another noun or pronoun between the *ce que* and the next verb), e.g.

  Tu me demandes ce que je fais le matin.
  You ask me what I do in the morning.

- *ce dont* is used when the literal meaning of what you want to say is "that of which", "that of what", e.g.

  Dis-moi ce dont tu as besoin.
  Tell me what you need.
  Ce dont j'ai besoin, c'est une voiture!
  What I need is a car!

If learning these rules of grammar is giving you a migraine, just memorize the phrases above instead. You may find that you can use them in your writing and that you can adapt them to say other things too.

- *Lequel, laquelle, lesquels, lesquelles* – which can also mean "who", "whom" and "that" – are usually used after a preposition, e.g.

  preposition

  Voici l'hôtel devant lequel j'ai vu le fantôme d' Elvis Presley!
  There is the hotel in front of which I saw Elvis Presley's ghost!

Not surprisingly, the form of *lequel* you use has to agree with the gender and number of the noun you are referring back to, e.g.

feminine plural

feminine plural form of lequel

Regardez <u>les personnes</u> avec <u>lesquelles</u> je travaille!
Look at the people I work with! (with whom I work).

TOP TIP

Never plonk a preposition, such as *avec*, at the end of a clause. Always put it in front of the *qui/lequel/laquelle*, etc., e.g.

Je n'oublierai jamais les clowns avec qui j'ai travaillé.
I will never forget the clowns I worked with.

- When *lequel*, *laquelle*, etc. are used with *à* or *de* they become *auquel* or *duquel*, etc.

   Ce sont des choses dans la garde-robe de Tonia Ravonia auxquelles elle ne pense pas!
   There are things in Tonia Ravonia's wardrobe she doesn't think about!

Mini word kit
penser à = to think about

Exam battle plan
The good news about your reading exam is that you won't need to understand every single word of the text to answer the questions. To gain a Grade C you simply have to show the examiners that you can recognize details and points of view from texts. And to

gain a Grade A you have to show them that you can also recognize attitudes and emotions and draw conclusions.

If you're in need of an exam battle plan to help you find the answers you want from fairly long exam texts, here's what you're looking for:

1. Before you so much as glance at the main text, read the introduction and questions. This will help you focus on the information you need to look for to answer the questions.

2. Skim-read the text.

3. Go through each question in turn and match it roughly with the part of the text containing the answer. Put a line beside, or under, each chosen part of the text and number it, so that you can find it again quickly when you move on to the next step. If you can't match a question with its answer, move on. Questions usually appear in the same order as the information in the text so you should be able to find any "unknown" answers at the end from the gaps in your marking scheme.

4. Read the text carefully to find out the exact answers to the questions.

5. Try to work out what unknown words mean from the sentence or paragraph they are in. If you look at a word in context you stand more chance of making a sensible guess as to its meaning than if you look at it on its own.

6. If a question asks for an overall impression, look through the whole text for clues before you come up with your answer.

7. Check that your responses answer the questions. If the question is in English, answer in English. If it's in French, answer in French. If there's a number in brackets after the question, this tells you how many marks will be awarded for that question, so make sure you write down the corresponding number of points/details.

But note . . .
If the text uses the *je* or *nous* forms of verbs, you will probably have to use the *il/elle* or *ils/elles* form of the same verbs to answer the questions, e.g.

> Text: ***Je fais** du surf tous les jours.*
> Question: *Qu'est-ce qu'**elle fait** tous les jours?*
> Answer: ***Elle fait** du surf.*

Remember, if your answers sound ridiculous or don't make sense, they can't be correct.

For revision tips, see page 189.

TOP TIP
You can brush up your skim-reading skills by timing yourself for 15 seconds as you skim-read newspaper articles in English. When your 15 seconds are up, test yourself to see how much you have understood.

Exam battle plan in action
On the next page is a short summary of a film no one in their right mind would go to see. Read the questions first, then skim-read the summary, before continuing with this chapter.

> **Virginie Vee, voleuse de poissons, entre dans un supermarché, prend des sardines gelées du congélateur, les met dans son soutien-gorge et s'évanouit du froid. Quand elle se réveille, elle se trouve dans un hôpital. Là, elle rencontre Jean-Michel,**

un médecin aux mains chaudes qu'elle connaissait quand elle était jeune fille. Virginie n'aimait pas Jean-Michel quand ils étaient tous les deux enfants car il avait le visage boutonneux. Heureusement, il ne souffre plus en ce moment de ses boutons donc Virginie se décide à abandonner sa carrière comme voleuse de poissons et à l'épouser. Ils achètent un restaurant de fruits de mer près de la mer et ils vivent toujours heureux.

Question time!

1. What does Virginie Vee hide in her bra? (2)

2. Where does Virginie meet Jean-Michel again? (1)

3. What does Virginie decide to do when she meets Jean-Michel? (3)

4. What do Virginie and Jean-Michel buy? (2)

5. Would you pay good money to see this film? (0)

OK. Now here's the same summary again, but this time with scribbles made by a student who has tried to answer the questions by following the battle plan outlined on page 129.

Virginie Vee, voleuse de poissons, entre dans un

supermarché, prend des sardines gelées du

I know "geler" means "to freeze" so guess this means "frozen".

132

congélateur, les met dans son soutien-gorge et

Not sure what this means, but ↑
guess from Question 1, it means "bra".

s'évanouit du froid. Quand elle se réveille, elle se

↑ Haven't the faintest idea what this means, but
don't need to know to answer the question, so I'll
skip it.

2

trouve dans un hôpital. Là, elle rencontre Jean-

↑

"re" at the start of a verb often means "again",
so guess from Question 2 that this means
"meets again".

*Michel, un médecin aux mains chaudes qu'elle
connaissait quand elle était jeune fille. Virginie
n'aimait pas Jean-Michel quand ils étaient tous les
deux enfants car il avait le visage boutonneux.*

↑

Haven't the foggiest. Can see it's some sort of
adjective though because it describes "visage".
Hang on! I don't need to know its meaning
to answer the question, so what am I
bothering about?

Heureusement, il ne souffre plus en ce moment de ses

3

boutons donc Virginie se décide à abandonner

↑

"to abandon"? makes sense in this context.

sa carrière comme voleuse de poissons et à

↑   ↑

"career"? Makes sense   Umm! I know "voler" is
as "career". I'll go   "to steal" & "euse" shows
with "career".   it's a woman, so I'll opt
                           for "thief" (feminine).

4

l'épouser. Ils achètent un restaurant de fruits de mer

↑

A verb with a pronoun in front?

près de la mer et ils vivent toujours heureux.

Question time!

1. What does Virginie Vee hide in her bra? (2)
Frozen sardines.

2. Where does Virginie meet Jean-Michel again? (1)
In the hospital.

3. What does Virginie decide to do when she meets Jean-Michel? (3)
She abandons her career as a fish thief and marries him.

4. What do Virginie and Jean-Michel buy? (2)
A seafood restaurant.

5. Would you pay good money to see this film? (0)
No way.

Obviously it would be crazy to jot down every thought/query that runs through your head in the exam as this student has done here, but his thought processes and the way he's quickly worked out whereabouts in the text the answers lie are sound, so use them as a guide when you tackle the following exercises. Both texts come from magazines aimed at teenagers, but the first text is a bit easier than the second.

(If this is a library book, do the decent thing and write your answers on a separate piece of paper! There's nothing worse than getting geared up to fill in a questionnaire only to discover someone has beaten you to it!)

PETIT TEST PART ONE

- *Lisez cet article et répondez en français aux questions suivantes.*

(Only look up words you really need to know to answer the questions and use your common sense to work out others.)

MANGER: DANGER ou PLAISIR

En 1997 un nouveau danger a fait la Une des journaux: une bactérie, l'E-Coli 0157 (Escherichia Coli), qui se cache parfois dans la nourriture et qui est très dangereuse pour les enfants et les personnes âgées. Il y a eu plusieurs cas célèbres liés à l'E-Coli à travers le monde:

– En Ecosse, plusieurs personnes âgées sont mortes après avoir consommé de la viande contaminée.

– Au Japon, des centaines d'écoliers ont été malades après avoir mangé un repas de cantine contaminé.

– Enfin, aux États-Unis, l'E-Coli a été découvert dans des milliers de steaks hachés surgelés vendus dans les supermarchés et utilisés par les fast-food pour faire des hamburgers. Il y a chaque année, aux États-Unis, environ 20,000 personnes contaminées par l'E-Coli et plus de 200 morts liées à cette bactérie. Mais

135

la bonne nouvelle, c'est qu'il suffit de bien cuire les aliments pour tuer l'E-Coli.

<u>Autres dangers</u>

– La salmonelle se trouve surtout dans les poulets et les œufs (et par conséquent dans les produits fabriqués à base d'œufs comme par exemple les glaces).

– La listéria touche les produits laitiers comme le fromage et les yaourts.

– L'hépatite, une maladie du foie, peut se transmettre par des aliments mal lavés.

1. Pour qui est-ce que l'E-Coli est très dangereux?

_____(2)

(Make sure you understand the question. Remember key word/s in the question often appear in the text, e.g. "est très dangereux/ dangereuse". There are two marks for this question so write down two types of people.)

2. Combien d'écoliers ont été malades après avoir mangé l'E-Coli au Japon?

(If you don't know the phrase "combien de" look it up now and learn it. You should be scanning the text for a number.)

_____(1)

3. Combien de personnes sont mortes après avoir été contaminées par L'E-Coli aux États-Unis?

(Don't write out a full sentence. Just state the number.)
(Look for a form of the verb "mourir" in the text as well as other key words, e.g. États-Unis.)

_____(1)

4. Que doit-on faire pour détruire l'E-Coli?

_____(2)

(You might be able to guess the meaning of "détruire". What English verb does it remind you of?)
(Start your answer with "On doit . . .")

5. Écrivez trois aliments dans lesquels il se peut qu'on trouve la salmonelle.

_____(3)

(You need to give three bits of information.)

Answers on page 221.

PETIT TEST PART TWO

• Read this article about drugs and answer the questions in English.

(Only look up words you really need to know to answer the questions and use your common sense to work out others.)

LA DROGUE EN FRANCE

Un toxicomane est une personne qui utilise régulièrement des drogues dont on devient dépendant, telles que la cocaïne ou l'héroïne. Au départ, les raisons qui poussent un individu à utiliser de la drogue sont multiples: il peut s'agir d'un jeune qui veut essayer quelque chose d'interdit par curiosité ou sous la pression de ses amis, d'un chômeur qui veut oublier ses problèmes et qui trouve dans la drogue un moyen de fuite, d'un professionnel à succès qui veut lutter contre le stress, etc. De fait, il n'existe pas un modèle de toxicomanie mais bien des milliers de cas différents. Leur point commun? Une dépendance à des substances extrêmement dangereuses pour la santé et dont l'utilisation et la vente sont illégales en France.

Santé

Les toxicomanes sont confrontés à deux grands types de risques. Le premier est un risque immédiat associé à l'utilisation de certaines drogues dont les effets peuvent se manifester après un seul usage. Il s'agit souvent de réactions violentes comme des hallucinations, asphyxie, coma, hémorragie cérébrale, crise cardiaque, etc. Le deuxième est un risque dérivé qui vient de l'usage de certaines drogues. Les toxicomanes qui partagent leurs seringues courent, par exemple, un risque très élevé de contracter le virus du sida ou de l'hépatite. De plus, la consommation de drogues tend à attaquer le système immunitaire et à provoquer des problèmes mentaux qui peuvent pousser à la folie ou au suicide. Enfin, les drogues telles que le crack peuvent déclencher des comportements violents et celles qui font halluciner, comme les solvants ou l'ecstasy, sont la cause d'accidents parfois mortels.

1. What is a drug addict? (2)

2. Give three reasons why, according to this article, someone might turn to drugs. (3)

3. Name two side-effects that can occur after using drugs just once. (2)

4. What extra risks face drug addicts who inject? (2)

5. Why can drugs which cause hallucinations be particularly harmful? (2)

Answers on page 222.

138

TOP TIP

If you're reading/listening to something and you're not sure whether the future tense is being used, look/listen to see/hear whether there is an **r** just before the end of the verb. If there is, you're probably in the future, e.g. *je parlerai*, I will talk. (See page 14 to see how the future tense is formed and pages 201 to 210 to see what irregular verbs look like in the future tense.)

TOP TIP II

If you're doing Foundation level reading, make sure you can recognize the present, perfect, imperfect and future tenses. And if you're doing Higher level, make sure you recognize all the tenses, including the pluperfect!

Pourriez-vous répéter, mate?

Listening practice

The most exciting way to improve your listening skills is to go to France and speak the lingo. However, if an imminent trip to France is about as likely as your parents giving you the keys to their cocktail cabinet, *panique pas*! Tuning into French radio or watching some French satellite TV every day will also help you sharpen up your listening skills.* Chances are you won't understand a lot of what you hear, but don't let that put you off. Just listen out for the words you do understand and use them to make an intelligent guess at the meaning of the rest. If your brain can take the strain, pay particular attention to any chat where there are interruptions, background noise or two people talking at once. The recording used in your final exam will contain a bit of background noise and natural features of speech.

Other listening resources you could check out include French films on TV and/or video – the subtitles will help you follow what's going on – and TV and radio programmes aimed at French learners. Ask your teacher if s/he has recordings of these you can use.

*If your school has satellite TV, why not ask whether French programmes can be recorded and made available to you?

...Et maintenant, vous allez entendre une conversation entre deux personnes qui aiment parler en même temps.

...And now, you are going to hear a conversation between two people who like to talk at the same time.

TOP TIP
Try to listen to French people speaking formally as well as informally. A variety of ways of speaking may be included in your final exam so listen to as many different types of speakers as possible.

TOP TIP II
Learn your set vocab! If you are familiar with the words that are likely to crop up in reading exercises/exams, you can't go far wrong.

Dowdy Dion
Agony Aunt
Miel Magazine
Rue du Rhum
Montpellier

Dear Dowdy,

Why is it that every time I tune into French radio or listen to a French tape in class the recording sounds like it's playing too fast? By the time I've worked out the first unknown word, the programme/tape has come to an end!

Yours, frustrated,

Deidre

Chère Deidre,

Zuh reason you are 'aving problems understanding spoken French eez because your brain eez not processing zuh information eet eez receiving quickly enough. In ah-zaire words, you need to improve your ability to retain information for as long as eet takes your brain to decode eet (either zat or you need a French brain). One technique guaranteed to 'elp you improve zis ability eez "The Six-Point Plan to Easy Listening" which I am enclosing.

Amitiés,

Dowdy

The six-point plan to easy listening

Step 1. Beg, borrow or buy a listening resource with a written copy of what's being said.

Step 2. Listen to a short sentence and try to repeat it in your head in French.

Step 3. Write down the words in French as you try to work out what they mean.

Step 4. Listen to the sentence again and check your interpretation with the written material.

Step 5. Repeat steps **2–4** with the next part of the tape.

Step 6. Gradually increase the amount you can listen to and understand at once.

Step 7. There is no step **7**. That's why it's called *The Six-Point Plan*.

There are a number of text books and listening resources which come with French cassettes – *Etincelle* published by Authentik, for example – so your best bet is to pop into a good bookshop or a well-stocked public library and see what you can find. Better still, ask your teacher for help. It will make him or her as happy as a hog to know that you want to do extra work!

One of your French students wants extra work?!

Listening tips

Chances are whatever kind of aural practice you do, you will sometimes feel that what you are listening to makes about as much sense as your gran after a night on the sherry. To help yourself make more sense of the sounds, try to remember the following:

- The consonant at the end of a word is rarely pronounced. HOWEVER, if the word following starts with a vowel or **h**, the two words run together and sound like one, e.g. *petit oiseau* is pronounced "purtee̲twa-zoe". If you remember this as you try to split up the sounds, they should start to make more sense.

- Generally, an **-s** at the end of a word is silent, but when the next word begins with a vowel or **h**, it is pronounced, e.g. *je suis* is pronounced "zhuh swee" but *je suis ici* is pronounced "zhuh swee̲z ee-see". Don't let this joining together of words throw you.

- The stress in a sentence tends to fall on the last syllable of a group of words, so keep your ears peeled for the change to help you make sense of the sentence.

- The endings of verbs let you know their tense and therefore their meaning, so it's worth listening out particularly carefully for them.

(For lots more about French sounds and how they are pronounced, see page 172.)

Exam battle plan

As with your reading exam, the great thing about your GCSE listening exam, and the listening tests you do in class for that matter, is that you don't have to understand every single word spoken in order to answer the questions.

To help you pick out the information you want, all you really need do is:

1. First read the question set, make sure you understand it and underline any key words, if appropriate.

2. Use the question and any visuals to help you anticipate some of the vocab that might crop up in the passage.

3. Listen out carefully for the words you need to answer the question and don't worry about the rest. You may find it useful to take short notes during the first playing of the passage and then write your answers during and after the second playing.

4. Answer the question fully, but don't waste time writing out complete sentences. For example, if the question asks *pourquoi est-ce que Marco est triste?* just write why he is sad, not *Marco est triste parce que* . . .

5. Look at the number of marks in brackets and make sure you make the corresponding number of points. If you are asked to mention two items, however, and you know three, write down all three. If you are asked to give times or measurements, make sure you specify the time of day or the unit of measurement.

TOP TIP
Times and numbers are really popular in listening exams so make sure you can identify them. Being able to understand the alphabet in French and common abbreviations, such as SNCF, P et T and RER, is important too.

For a pronunciation guide to the French alphabet, see page 176.

For revision tips, see page 189.

One final point before your brain cracks up due to information overload! Don't be an idiot and skive off any mock exams or listening exercises your teacher does with you using past papers. Answering questions in a booklet while listening to speech on a tape is not a normal activity (at least not for most of us) and is therefore something that needs plenty of practice.

How do you write right in French?

The key to a successful piece of GCSE writing is to <u>plan</u> what you are going to write before you commit pen to paper. That way you can make sure you give yourself plenty of opportunity to show off what you know and can do. Here's the sort of thing you might be asked to do:

> *Écrivez une lettre à votre nouveau correspondant français. Parlez-lui du travail que vous faites pour gagner de l'argent.*

A good plan for your letter might go something like this:

- Say that I have a Saturday job.
- Say what my job involves: where I work, what I do, who I work with, whether I like my work, what hours I work, how much I am paid and whether I think it's enough.
- Say what job I did last year and what I thought about it.
- Say what my immediate plans are.
- Say what my future employment plans are.
- Ask about my pen pal's job/hobbies.

OK, so a letter along these lines won't exactly have your pen pal begging for a sequel, but it will be well constructed, with a beginning, middle and an end, and it will give you plenty of opportunities to refer to things that happened in the past as well as things that will happen in the future. This is important, as your teacher/examiner will be incredibly impressed if you use a variety of verb tenses accurately. He/she will also go dippy with delight if you express a personal opinion in your writing, so saying what you think about your Saturday job will bump up your grade.

Strut your stuff!

Like the grooviest dancing, the best GCSE writing is about showing off. So don't just shuffle along choosing the easiest words and sentence structures you can think of. Leap into action by taking these tips instead:

- Avoid starting every sentence with *je*. If you don't, you'll bore the blisters off your reader.

- Go for flow whenever you can. For example, instead of writing "*Je travaille dans une boulangerie. Elle se situe à Doncaster,*" write "*Je travaille dans une boulangerie **qui** se situe à Doncaster.*"

Remember, size does matter when it comes to GCSE sentences, so use linking words to help lengthen yours such as *et*, *parce que*, *puis*, *donc*. (See pages 89 and 90 for more about *qui*, *que* and *dont*, and linking words.)

- Pepper your writing with prepositions: ***après*** *mes examens,* ***derrière*** *la maison,* ***en face de*** *mon lit.* Make sure you have a stock of them in your head before you go into your final exam. (See page 79 for more about prepositions.)

- Instead of repeating a noun you've already used, dazzle and delight by using a pronoun! In other words, don't write "*Hier j'ai vu un film. J'ai vu le film avec mon ami, Vernon.*" Go wild and put "*Hier j'ai vu un film. Je l'ai vu avec mon ami, Vernon.*" (See pages 70–78 for the lowdown on pronouns.)

- Use a variety of verbs and, if possible, try to include a few that are followed by an infinitive, e.g.

  Il a commencé à travailler.
  He began to work.

  Je voudrais rester.
  I would like to stay.

  Pouvez-vous m'aider?
  Can you help me?

- Try to avoid using English words such as *Coronation Street* and *EastEnders*.

- Remember to say what you think about something whenever you can. One way to do this is to use *c'est* if you are talking about the present; *c'était* if you are talking about the past; and *ce sera* if you are talking about the future.

  C'est nul.　　　　　　　*C'était intéressant.*
  It is rubbish.　　　　　It was interesting.

  C'est ennuyeux.　　　　*C'était super.*
  It is boring.　　　　　 It was great.

  Ce sera délicieux.　　　*Ce sera facile.*
  It will be delicious.　　It will be easy.

149

- Pump up the detail whenever you can by using words such as these:

très	very	*beaucoup*	a lot, very much
pas très	not very		
assez de	enough	*pas beaucoup*	not a lot
tout à fait	completely	*tellement*	so
trop de	too much	*tant*	so much
peu	little	*presque*	nearly, almost
un peu	a little	*tout*	all
plutôt	rather	*vraiment*	really

Secret thoughts of the examiner

Common words like *bon* and *très* are fine and dandy, but not when they appear in every other sentence. So if you're doing Higher-level writing, please, do me a favour and use some more unusual alternatives instead. For example, instead of saying "*Je suis très heureux/heureuse car . . .*" you could say "*Je suis tellement heureux/heureuse car . . .*" Now, that would really impress me.

The key point to remember when it comes to GCSE writing is to try to use as many verb tenses as accurately as you can. (For more about verbs, see chapter 1.) The words/phrases on the next couple of pages will help you refer to different tenses.

Talking about the future

Tomorrow   *Demain*

> *Demain soir, je vais aller au cinéma mais mardi je vais jouer au tennis.*
> Tomorrow evening I am going to go to the cinema but on Tuesday I am going to play tennis.

Next   *Prochain*

> *Le week-end prochain j'irai en ville et l'année prochaine j'achèterai une voiture.*
> Next weekend I will go into town and next year I will buy a car.

Talking about the past

Yesterday   *Hier*

> *Hier après-midi je suis allé(e) au théâtre.*
> Yesterday afternoon I went to the theatre.

The day before yesterday *Avant-hier*

> *Avant-hier, il a regardé un match de football.*
> The day before yesterday he watched a football match.

Last   *Dernier*

> *Mardi dernier j'ai joué au ping-pong; le week-end dernier j'ai visité un musée; et l'année dernière, j'ai cherché un emploi en France.*

151

Last Tuesday I played ping-pong; last weekend I visited a museum; and last year I looked for a job in France.

During   *Pendant*

Pendant les vacances j'ai été à la plage tous les jours.
During the holidays I went to the beach every day.

Ago   *Il y a*

Son chien est mort il y a une semaine.
His dog died a week ago.

Talking about the present

On Sundays   *Le dimanche*

Je sors le dimanche.
I go out on Sundays.

In the evenings   *Le soir*

Je fais la vaisselle le soir.
In the evenings, I do the dishes.

At weekends   *Le week-end*

D'habitude, le week-end, je rencontre mes amis.
Usually I meet my friends at weekends.

PETIT TEST

While your brain is still buzzing with writing tips, grab a piece of paper and jot down the following:

1. A brief opinion to go with each of these sentences.

Exemple:

> *Hier soir j'ai regardé mon émission préférée.*
> ***C'était superbe.***
> Yesterday evening I watched my favourite programme. **It was superb.**

a) *Avant-hier, j'ai regardé un film.*
b) *J'adore le chocolat chaud.*
c) *Demain, nous allons visiter un musée.*
d) *La semaine dernière, nous avons fait une excursion à Grimsdale.*

2. An explanation to complete these opinions.

Exemple:

> *Je n'aime pas la ville dans laquelle j'habite parce qu'il n'y a rien à faire.*
> I don't like the town I live in because **there is nothing to do.**

a) *J'adore la biologie parce que . . .*
b) *Je déteste l'anglais parce que . . .*
c) *Je préfère passer les grandes vacances dans un pays chaud parce que . . .*
d) *Je voudrais travailler dans une confiserie parce que . . .*

153

3. A translation for each of these sentences.

Last summer I worked in a supermarket that was near the town centre. It was awful and I didn't earn a lot of money.

Next summer I will go to France and work in a café. I have already been to France and I really liked my holidays there.

At the moment I am revising for my exams. I have a lot of homework and I don't like that. For example, last weekend I stayed in my room and spent all my time working. I was so bored!

Answers on page 222.

Secret thoughts of the examiner

If you're aiming for a Grade A in your writing exam, here's a selection of phrases that, if used accurately, will help you achieve your goal and will warm the cockles of my heart into the bargain!

- *après* + *avoir/être* + past participle* means "after having done something".

*In case you've forgotten, the past participle is the part of a verb that is used with *avoir* or *être* to form the perfect tense.

Après avoir fait les courses, Madame Brown est allée à Paris.
After having done the shopping, Mrs Brown went to Paris.

If you use an *être* verb in your writing (which you should try to do), remember to add an extra **-e** to the past participle if the person/thing doing the action is feminine, and **-s** if there is more than one person/thing doing the action.

155

Après être arrivée en France, Madame Brown a fait les courses.
After arriving in France, Mrs Brown did some shopping.

- *en* + the present participle (the part of the verb that is expressed by **-ing** in English) means "when/by/on doing . . ."

*Cherie s'est cassé le bras **en** jouant au Tiddlywinks.*
Cherie broke her arm while playing Tiddlywinks.

The present participle can also be used on its own.

> **Voyant** que Cherie était blessée, son père a remis le jeu à sa place.
> Seeing that Cherie was wounded, her father put away the game.

- *sans* + infinitive means "without doing . . ."

Sans hésiter, Cyril a cédé son siège.
Without hesitating, Cyril gave up his seat.

- *avant de* + infinitive means "before doing . . ."

  Avant de *quitter la maison, Danielle a verifié son reflet dans le miroir.*
  Before leaving the house, Danielle checked her reflection in the mirror.

- present tense of a verb + *depuis* means "to have done something for a period of time".

  *J'habite à Grimsby **depuis** 10 ans.*
  I have lived in Grimsby for 10 years.

158

- One of the best ways to say what you were doing when something else happened is to use the imperfect tense of *être en train de* + an infinitive.

  > **J'étais en train de** *traverser la rue quand j'ai vu un accident.*
  > I was crossing the road when I saw an accident.

TOP TIP

If you want your writing grade/s to rocket through the roof, don't just give your opinion about things, give your reasons for those opinions too, e.g.

Je préfère le dessin parce que c'est plus intéressant que l'histoire.
I prefer art because it is more interesting than history.

A mon avis c'est un bon feuilleton parce qu'il est rigolo.
In my opinion it is a good serial because it is funny.

- Getting to grips with the pronouns y and en takes time and patience, but if you can suss out how to use them correctly, you'll achieve star student status!
  Like other object pronouns, both y and en go before the verb (see page 75). Y means "there" when you are talking about a place you're at or are going to, e.g.

  > *Décrivez votre ville et dites si vous aimez **y** habiter.*
  > Describe your town and say if you like living there.

159

Y is also often used to replace *à* + noun, when the noun refers to a thing or a place.

Tu penses au gâteau au chocolat? Are you thinking about chocolate cake?

J'y pense sans cesse. I think about it all the time.

En can mean "some", "any", "it", "them", "of it" or "of them" and usually replaces *de* + a noun that refers to a thing or place.

Speech bubble (left): *Tu te souviens de ta première bise?* Do you remember your first kiss?

Speech bubble (right): *Oui, je m'en souviens très bien!* Yes, I remember it very well!

Mini word kit

Se souvenir de quelque chose = to remember something

TOP TIP

The phrase *il y a* (there is/there are) is a handy one, but *il y avait* (there was/were) is more unusual and therefore more impressive, so use it when you can! Remember all the other useful variations of *il y a* too, e.g.

y a-t-il?	is there?/are there?
n'y a-t-il pas?	isn't there?/aren't there?
il y a eu	there has been

PETIT TEST

Using a bit of scrap paper, see if you can translate the following into French.

1. Cher ami

You ask what I did this morning. I got up at 7.30 as usual, I washed and got dressed. Before leaving the house I had breakfast – some tea and toast. After eating [i.e. after having eaten] I went out to catch the train to school.

On arriving at school, I met my friend Joey and we chatted for a few minutes. Our first lesson began at nine o'clock exactly. It was quite interesting!

And you, what do you do in the mornings when you are going to school? Do you have to get up early? Next Saturday I am going to stay in bed all day!

Write soon.

2.
- I have never visited Brazil but I would like to go there one day.
- I have lived in Birmingham for fifteen years and I like living there.
- We went to Scotland two years ago and it was great.
- I was in the middle of parking the car when an ambulance collided with the old lady.
- There has been an accident. Is there a doctor here?

● How many horror films have you seen? I've seen twenty-nine!

Answers on page 223.

Secret thoughts of the examiner

If you're aiming for a Grade A in your final writing exam, you need to show me that you've got a good range of vocab and phrases up your sleeve and that you know how to put sentences together in different ways. Your coursebook may well have a list of words and phrases to help you jazz up your narratives, articles or stories. Get to know these and the words and phrases over the page and then include them in your writing whenever you can. That way you'll gain the confidence to use them in your final writing exam.

à ce moment-là . . .	at that moment
à ma grande surprise . . .	to my astonishment
sans perdre du temps . . .	without wasting time
tandis que . . .	while
tout à coup . . .	suddenly
tout de suite . . .	immediately
peu à peu . . .	gradually
tout d'abord . . .	at first, first of all
surtout . . .	especially, above all
alors . . .	then, so
après cela . . .	after that
après un certain temps . . .	after a while
enfin . . .	at last
pour la première fois . . .	for the first time
à l'heure . . .	on time
peu de temps après . . .	a short time later
plus tard que d'habitude . . .	later than usual
dès maintenant . . .	from now on
cependant . . .	however
c'est-à-dire . . .	that is to say
de toute façon . . .	anyway
en effet . . .	as a matter of fact
en fait . . .	in fact
heureusement . . .	fortunately
malheureusement . . .	unfortunately
quand même . . .	all the same

Chère Cherie . . .

OK, so when it comes to letter writing it's what you put in the letter that counts most. However, if you begin with the wrong spelling of *Cher/Chère* and end with something totally inappropriate, you won't exactly make a fabulous impression, so don't lose valuable marks by ignoring the following.

1. When writing to a male mate of your own age, you should begin your letter with *Cher* + the name of your mate, or *Cher ami*. If you are writing to a female friend, you begin with *Chère* + her name, or *Chère amie*. And if you are writing to a group of pals you could begin with *Chers amis*. You put the name of your town and the date at the top right-hand side of the letter, and if you are writing to someone your own age you use the *tu* form of the verb to address them, e.g.

Lyons, le 6 mars 2002

Chère Michelle,

Je te remercie de ta dernière lettre. Excuse-moi de ne pas avoir écrit plus tôt mais la semaine dernière des extra-terrestres m'ont enlevé et ils m'ont transporté chez eux . . .

Lyons, 6 March 2002

Dear Michelle,

Thank you for your last letter. I apologize for not writing to you earlier but last week I was abducted by some aliens and taken back to their home . . .

If you want to add a neat closing phrase before you sign off, you could put something like . . .

Maintenant je vais te quitter car je dois faire mes devoirs/je dois nettoyer la cuisine/je dois escalader le mur.
Now I'm going to leave you because I must do my homework/clean the kitchen/climb the wall.

Mes parents te disent un petit bonjour.
My parents say hi.

En attendant tes nouvelles . . .
Looking forward to hearing your news . . .

2. To finish off your letter you could write *Amitiés* – Kind regards; or À *bientôt* – See you soon; or, if you're feeling very frisky, *Grosses bises* – Lots of kisses.

3. If you are asked to write *une lettre formelle*, in response to a job advert for example, forget about *cher/chère*. Instead begin with one of the following –

Monsieur	Dear Sir
Madame	Dear Madame
Messieurs	Dear Sirs

– and finish with

Je vous prie d'agréer, Madame/Monsieur, l'expression de mes sentiments distingués.

which is a long-winded way of saying "Yours sincerely/faithfully". Don't forget to address the person you are talking to as *vous* throughout.

Pick up a postcard

Should you be asked to write a postcard, here are some snappy
expressions you may find useful:

Salut! Hi!

Me voici en vacances à... Here I am on holiday at/in...
Il fait beau/chaud/froid. The weather is fine/hot/cold. *Je
m'amuse beaucoup.* I'm having a great time. *Je me
baigne/je fais du ski/je fais de la planche à voile
tous les jours.* I swim/ski/windsurf every day. *L'hôtel a
les vues superbes.* The hotel has fabulous views. *Le
camping est formidable.* The campsite is great. *Le chien
a eu la diarrhée.* The dog had diarrhoea. (Just checking
you're paying attention!)

À bientôt. See you soon.

Check it write!

When you've finished a piece of GCSE writing you should always
check it through and ask yourself the following:

Verbs

✔ Are all my verbs in the correct tense?
✔ Do the endings "agree with" the subjects (the *je, tu, il,* etc.)?
✔ In the perfect tense, have I used *avoir* and *être* with the
correct verbs?
✔ With *être* verbs, do the past participles have the correct endings?*

*See page 20 for rules about verb agreement with a preceding direct object.

Nouns
✔ Have I put the correct sort of word in front: i.e. *le, la, l'* or *les; de, de l', du, de la* or *des?*

Adjectives
✔ Have I added **-e** to adjectives describing feminine nouns, **-s** to adjectives describing masculine plural nouns, and **-es** to adjectives describing feminine plural nouns?
✔ Have I put the adjective in the right place?
✔ Have any irregular adjectives been spelt correctly?

General
✔ Have I put my accents the right way round?
✔ Is my handwriting easy to read?
✔ Will this ever-growing checklist ever come to an end?

It's worth making the effort to keep your handwriting neat and legible, as trying to decipher sheet after sheet of sloppy scribble would try the patience of a corpse, never mind a teacher or examiner!

> **TOP TIP**
> Always check any corrected work you get back from your teacher. Make a list of all the errors you make on a regular basis so that you can go over them before the final exam.

PETIT TEST

While working as a hotel receptionist in Nice, you receive this letter from someone wanting to stay in the hotel. Unfortunately the letter contains eleven *erreurs affreuses*. Can you identify all eleven? Your time limit starts . . . now!

Leeds, le 6 mars 2001

Madame/Monsieur,

J'ai l'intention de passer quelques jours à Nice au mois de septembre. Avait-vous de chambre libre du 1 au 4 septembre? Je voudrais réserver un grand chambre pour une personne avec mini-bar. Je suis un chien vieux. Vous permettons aux animals de loger dans votre hôtel?

On m'a dis que les restaurants dans l'hôtel sont les plus bons de Nice. C'était vrai? Et le chef, préparera-t-il des repas pour les animaux?

Je vous prie d'agréer, Madame/Monsieur, l'expression de mes sentiments distingués.

Wally Weeve

Answers on page 224.

Now have a go at adapting this letter so that it asks for a double room with a shower for the 12–14 of April instead of a single room with a mini-bar. Also, instead of asking whether the chef caters for animals, ask what time dinner is served. If you get stuck, look at the model letter on page 224.

Exam battle plan

As with all the other skills, it's vital that you find out from your teacher and/or the syllabus the sort of tasks you'll be expected to perform in your final writing exam, as well as the topic areas that will be covered. That way you will know exactly what best to revise.

On the day of the exam itself, your best strategy for success is to . . .

1. Read the questions very carefully and make sure you understand them. It's crucial that you do exactly what you've been asked to do.

2. Don't be tempted to start writing furiously from the word go, even if that's what everyone else seems to do. Plan each answer before you start to write. Remember, your aim is to show the examiner what you can do and that includes coming up with personal opinions where appropriate and, if at all possible, referring to the past, present and future using a variety of verbs. If faced with a long writing task, you might find it helpful to jot down the first sentence of each paragraph in your plan.

3. Make sure you complete all the tasks in each question. Yep, this sounds blindingly obvious, but exams can do funny things to people and even the brainiest candidates can (and do) throw away crucial marks by not writing something for every point required. One way to ensure you answer everything is to tick each point on the paper as you finish writing about it.

4. As far as possible, stick to using words and phrases that you could write in your sleep. The exam is not the ideal place to try out fancy new phrases you've just invented.

5. If you're doing Higher-level writing, see if you can add some extra information – an opinion or some extra details – to every statement you make.

6. When you've finished, run through the "Check it write" plan in your head and check your answers against it.

I have nothing to say about the oral!

8

Learning French pronunciation from a book is a bit like trying to watch telly with the sound turned down – ce n'est pas idéal!

The best way to learn how to make the sounds French people make is to listen to as much spoken French as you can and imitate what you hear. HOWEVER . . . if you're stuck at home with not a French speaker in sight and you need to check the pronunciation of a word or sound quickly, sound guides, like the one below, can be of help. The pronunciation pointers given in this guide, which are based on Standard English pronunciation, don't cover all French sounds though, so if you can't find what you're looking for here, check out the phonetic pronunciation guide in your French/English dictionary.

Pronunciation pointers
For best results, practise saying all the French words and phrases below <u>out loud</u>.

- **a** and **à** often sound like the **a** in c<u>a</u>t, e.g. *Le mari à Paris.*

- **é, er, ez, ai** and **ay** are pronounced like the **ay** sound in l<u>a</u>te, e.g.

172

> *Regardez le bébé.*
> Look at the baby.

- è, ê, and e, and **aient**, **ais**, **ait** and **aî** all sound like the e in v<u>e</u>t, e.g. *vous êtes*, *une chaîne*, but sometimes e is pronounced as **euh**, e.g. *je*, *le*, *regarder*.

- **ui** sounds like the English word **wee**, so *traduire* sounds like trahd<u>wee</u>r.

- **i** is often pronounced like the **ee** in f<u>ee</u>t, e.g.

> *Oui, mon père est Sicilien.*
> Yes, my dad is Sicilian.

and

> *Viens vite! Mon lit est en feu!*
> Come quick! My bed's on fire!

- **o** often sounds like the **o** in h<u>o</u>liday, e.g. *donner*.

- **oi** sounds like the **wha** in <u>wha</u>m, e.g. *poisson*, *boisson*.

- The letters **ou** sound like the **oo** in f<u>oo</u>d, e.g.

> *La roue roule sous le trou.*
> The wheel rolls under the hole.

(Hey! No one said these practice sentences had to make sense!)

- To pronounce the letter **u**, hold out your lips in a tight **O**, place the tip of your tongue near the top of your lower teeth and say **ew** as in y<u>ew</u> without moving your lips. Yes, you will look like a startled chimpanzee, but at least the noise you make should sound right. Words that include this sound are *du*, *une* and *plus*.

- **ch** is pronounced like the **sh** in s<u>h</u>ut, e.g.

  Chantal chante sa chanson.
  Chantal sings her song.

- **c** when used before **i** or **e** sounds like the **s** in <u>s</u>ee, e.g.

  Six cent scies et six cent citrons.
  Six hundred saws and six hundred lemons.

  When used before other letters, however, **c** sounds like the **c** in <u>c</u>rab, e.g.

  C'est <u>c</u>ombien ce <u>c</u>afé-ci?
  How much is this coffee?

- **ç** sounds like the **s** in <u>s</u>urf, e.g.

  Le garçon français s'est assis sur la chaise.
  The French boy sat down on the chair.

- **g** when used before **e**, **i** or **y** sounds soft like the **s** in plea<u>s</u>ure, e.g. *page, âge,* but before **a**, **o**, or **u** it sounds hard, like the **g** in good grief!, e.g. *gare, guitare.*

- **gn** sounds like the **ni** sound in o<u>ni</u>on, e.g. *campagne, montagne*.

- Neither **h** at the beginning of a word, nor **e** at the end of a word is pronounced, which is consistent if nothing else!

- **j** sounds like the **s** in trea<u>s</u>ure, e.g.

  Le juge est juste, jeune, juif et jaloux.
  The judge is fair, young, Jewish and jealous.

- The French sound for **n** comes from the back of the nose and is best practised by holding your nose, saying words such as *rien, un* and *non* and then trying to make the same sounds without the nose hold. If you sound like you're talking through your nose and mouth at the same time, you've got it!

- **qu** sounds like the **k** in kettle, e.g.

  Qu'est-ce que c'est la question?
  What's the question?

- The famous rolling **r** sound you hear in words such as *boire* and *gare*, is made by growling a little at the back of your throat. If you sound like you're gargling or choking, you're on the right lines.

- Both **t** and **th** are pronounced like the **t** in <u>t</u>ent, e.g.

  Trois tantes trottaient sur le trottoir.
  Three aunts were trotting down the pavement.

- **-tion** and **-sion** at the end of a word sound like "see-on", not "shon" as you might expect.

- **-ent** at the end of a word other than a verb sounds like **ong** without the g.

175

WARNING

Remember, a consonant at the end of a word is rarely pronounced, e.g. *lent* (slow). But if *-e* is added to the end, the consonant often *is* sounded, e.g. *lente* (feminine singular of *lent*).

TOP TIP

One easy way to sound French is to put a slight stress on the second syllable of a word, not the first, e.g. foot<u>ball</u> (not <u>foot</u>ball) and rug<u>by</u> (not <u>rug</u>by). For more about French stress (as if we haven't got enough of our own!) and the running together of words, see page 144.

The French alphabet

A – ah	B – bay	C – say
D – day	E – euh	F – eff
G – jay	H – ash	I – ee
J – jee	K – kah	L – el
M – em	N – en	O – oh
P – pay	Q – ku	R – air
S – es	T – tay	U – ou
V – vay	W – doublevay	
X – eex	Y – eegrec	Z – zed

176

The more you practise speaking French, the better your pronunciation and fluency will become, so seize every opportunity you get to chat in French or read out loud. You shouldn't have much trouble finding French to read out loud, but if you need a boot up the bum, here are a few tongue twisters and a short magazine article to get you started. Remember to pronounce the English words in the article with a French accent!

Les chaussettes de l'archi-duchesse, sont-elles sèches ou archi-sèches?
Are the socks of the archduchess dry or extra-dry?

Un chasseur sachant chasser doit chasser sans son chien de chasse.
A hunter who knows how to hunt must hunt without his hunting dog.

Une bête noire se baigne dans une baignoire noire.
A black beast bathes in a black bathtub.

Pendant ces dernières années, un grand nombre de mots anglais/américains est de plus en plus utilisé dans la langue française. C'est pourquoi les autorités françaises ont vite créé des équivalents français de mots et d'expressions anglais largement utilisés. Ainsi, on propose aux Français de remplacer "walkman" par "baladeur", "compact disc" par "disque audio-numérique", "video clip" par "bande promo", "jingle" par "sonal", "airbag" par "sac gonflable", pour ne citer que quelques mots. De même, une équipe de football ne bénéficie plus "d'un corner" mais "d'un jet de coin". On ne va plus voir "un one- man show" mais "un spectacle solo". Et un groupe de rock ne chante plus en "playback" mais "en présonorisation".

Exam preparation: acting up!

There's a lot you can do to prepare really well for your final speaking exam.

For role-plays, you can start by getting to know useful role-play expressions, like those below, and by practising the role-play situations you are likely to be tested on. Ask your teacher if you're not sure which role-play situations apply to your level of the exam and check your coursebook to see what useful role-play phrases it lists.

Get in role!

C'est combien…?	How much is it…?
Je voudrais…	I would like…
À quelle heure arrive/part le train/l'avion de…?	When does the train/ plane arrive/leave from…?
Excusez-moi…	Excuse me…
Attendez!	Wait!
Pouvez-vous me dire…?	Can you tell me…?
Pouvez-vous me dire où se trouve…?	Can you tell me where … is?

Pouvez-vous m'aider…?	Can you help me?
Pour aller à … s'il vous plaît?	How does one get to … please?
Y a-t-il…?	Is (are) there…?
Puis-je…?	May I…?
Je dois…	I must…
J'ai besoin de…	I need…
Je veux…	I want…
D'accord!	OK!
Je suis désolé(e)	I'm sorry
Formidable!	Great!
Entendu	Agreed
Quel dommage!	What a shame!
À ce soir	Till this evening
De rien, monsieur/madame!	Don't mention it!
	(i.e. no need to thank me)

For a reminder of how to form questions in French, see page 91.

The tasks you'll be expected to perform in the role-plays will be fairly straightforward, e.g.

You are arranging an afternoon out with a French friend.

- Suggest going for a walk.
- ! (*This means you'll have to respond to something not in your role-play instructions.*)
- Tell your friend where and when you will meet.
- Tell him/her you are going back to your house afterwards.

Your teacher will play the part of your French friend and will speak first.

Responding to something not in your role-play instructions isn't as scary as it sounds because the "unexpected" question you'll be asked isn't designed to trick you. For example, the unexpected question in the role-play above could well be something incredibly straightforward such as:

> *Quel temps fera-t-il cet après-midi?*
> **What will the weather be like this afternoon?**

to which you could reply:

> *D'après la météo, il fera beau.*
> **According to the weather forecast, it will be fine.**

or

> *Il fera beau.*
> **The weather will be fine.**

or

> *Il fera chaud.*
> **It will be hot.**

In addition to dealing with a task not in your role-play instructions, you might also have to cope with a "spanner-in-the-works" response. For example, if one of your tasks is to order something to eat in a restaurant and you choose steak and chips, your teacher may turn round and say:

> *Nous n'avons plus de steak.*
> **We don't have any more steak.**

Now, there are two ways of dealing with this sort of response. You can either clam up and look terror-stricken – which will score you *nul points*. Or you can show some initiative and say something like –

> *Alors, je prends le poisson avec des frites.*
> **Then, I'll have the fish and chips.**

– which will score you full points.

TOP TIP
When talking about food or drink in French, remember to use the verb *prendre* when you want to say "have".

If thinking on your feet doesn't come easy to you, plan ahead. For each role-play topic, think what questions the examiner might ask you and then prepare answers to those questions, including answers to "spanner-in-the-works" questions/responses. For example, if you're revising how to book accommodation, your first question might be:

> *Bonjour Monsieur/Madame. Avez-vous une chambre pour une personne avec douche?*

Now ask yourself, what might the reply be? It could be something straightforward such as –

> *Pour combien de nuits?*

– but there again it could be something really unhelpful such as –

> *Malheureusement, non.*

In which case you could reply:

Avez-vous une chambre avec salle de bains?

or

Il y a un autre hôtel près d'ici?

or

Is it too late to switch to German?

In short, prepare yourself for the unexpected! Write out conversations based on each topic you have to revise and learn your answers to the questions.

Preparation: presentation!

If you have to give a presentation for the exam, you should start preparing for it well in advance. That way you'll have plenty of time to rehearse it, and to try to anticipate the sorts of questions your teacher will ask so that you can prepare answers to those questions. When preparing your presentation, remember to:

a) Make it interesting, using as wide a variety of vocab and verb tenses as you can.
b) Keep it to the set time limit. This will probably be about a minute and a half, but double-check.
c) Prepare it as a series of mini-paragraphs. This will give you the flexibility of being able to move bits of your speech into the answers and vice versa. This is particularly useful if your brain suddenly shuts up shop and you forget parts of your speech!

Preparation: chit-chat

In the general conversation part of the exam, you'll be expected to chat with your teacher about topics such as • *Yourself, family and friends* • *Home and daily routine* • *Leisure* • *Your local area and*

abroad • *Holidays and tourism.* (As always, double-check that all these topic areas apply to you.)

Once you know which topics will be up for discussion, you can start anticipating the type of questions you are likely to be asked and preparing your answers. For example, if the topic area under examination is *Yourself, friends and family,* chances are you'll be asked questions like:

"Comment t'appelles-tu?"

"Quel âge as-tu?"

"Quelle est la date de ton anniversaire?"

"Quelle est ton adresse?" "Tu as des animaux?"

"Tu as des frères et des sœurs?"

"Tes parents, qu'est-ce qu'ils font dans la vie?"

183

In other words, think of questions you might reasonably be expected to answer for each topic area and prepare a response for each question! Don't settle for monosyllabic responses either. If you are an only child and your teacher/examiner asks: *"Tu as des frères et des sœurs?"* don't just say: *"Non"*. Either add a bit of extra information such as: *"Non, je suis enfant unique mais j'ai un chien et un chat"*, or tell a fib and announce you've got two brothers and four sisters and another on the way! The idea is to say as much as you can as accurately as you can. Should your teacher ever enquire as to why you've never spoken of your siblings before, tell him/her that they all spontaneously combusted after the exam!

As a general rule, your conversation replies should be at least one sentence long. However, since one of the main things you are being tested on is your ability to speak French accurately, using a variety of tenses and vocabulary, think about which questions lend themselves to longer answers and then practise your replies using as wide a range of vocab and verb tenses as you can. For example, if asked

Q. *Qu'est-ce que tu as fait samedi dernier?*

you could say

A. *Je suis allé(e) en ville et j'ai fait les magasins. J'ai acheté un pul rose. C'est très joli. Ce weekend je vais aller au théâtre avec mes parents.*

See how in just one answer you can refer to the past, present and future tenses and express a personal opinion! In your speaking exam, as in your writing exam, referring to the past, present and future and expressing opinions accurately will help bump up your grade.

If you are going for a top grade, you'll be expected to show that you can have a spontaneous conversation at some length, so your answers will need to be more detailed still, e.g.

Q. *Qu'est-ce que tu as fait le weekend dernier?*

A. *Alors, je me suis beaucoup amusé(e) le weekend dernier. Tout d'abord, samedi j'ai conduit en ville*

good use of adverb plus an opinion – lovely!

avec mes amis – c'était vraiment super, car c'était

l'anniversaire de mon meilleur ami, et on est allé ensemble au cinéma pour regarder un film

opinion... and reason for that opinion – brilliant!

d'épouvante. Je n'avais pas peur – au contraire, le film

était plutôt amusant! Après le film, nous sommes allés

correct use of a preposition – bliss!

manger dans un restaurant (près) du cinéma – un

restaurant italien – où j'ai rencontré une très jolie fille

avec qui j'ai parlé pendant des heures et des heures ...

etc., etc. Fabulous! Another good long sentence with lots of information in it & different types of words / grammatical constructions.

Overall: Good variety of verbs used, including a reflexive one & excellent use of the perfect and imperfect tenses. Fab!

It doesn't matter if what you say is a load of lies, so long as you answer the question, give lots of details and speak as fluently and accurately as possible with good pronunciation. Now, that's not too much to ask, is it?

(You'll find a list of useful descriptive words such as *vraiment* and *plutôt*, on page 150. In fact, many of the tips for improving your writing apply to your speaking, so be sure to read chapter 7.)

> **TOP TIP**
> Whatever kind of speaking task you are preparing for, put in some exam practice with a tape recorder running. The worst part of any exam is the stress of performing under pressure, so the more work you do under exam-like conditions, the better prepared you'll be for the stress.

Exam battle plan

If the very thought of your speaking exam is enough to make your heart stop as still as a comma in a coma, *panique pas*. Follow this speaking exam battle plan instead:

1. If you're doing a presentation, transfer any notes you are allowed to use on to postcards so that you can see at a glance what you want to say. Highlight key words and keep the text to a minimum.

2. Use the preparation period before the role-plays begin to try to anticipate what your teacher might ask you. If the role-play instructions give you short headings like this –

You go to a lost-property office at a French railway station to report the loss of your suitcase.

- *objet*
- *description* and *contenu*
- *où*
- !

186

– work out what you are going to say for each heading, e.g. *Objet: "J'ai perdu ma valise". Description: "Elle est assez grande et elle est rose et en cuir."* Only use your dictionary, if allowed, as a last resort.

The preparation period before the role-plays begin is also the ideal time to decide whether the character your teacher is playing should be addressed as *tu* or *vous*.

3. Once the exam begins, put into practice all you have learnt in this chapter. In the role-plays complete the tasks, replying in as much detail as possible. In the general conversation, pad out your answers with plenty of information. Now is not the time to do your impersonation of a clam!

> *Qu'as-tu l'intention de faire quand tu auras quitté cet examen?*

> *Rien. Je suis un clam!*

4. Watch yourself when it comes to verb tenses and forms; adjective agreements with a change of sound; genders; prepositions; and the agreement and order of pronouns. In other words, think carefully about everything you say. Your teacher wants to hear grammatically accurate French, not just a saucy accent!

5. If in doubt about which verb tense to use, mirror the tense used in the question, e.g. if you are asked a question in the perfect tense, answer in the perfect. You can always introduce other tenses later in your answer if appropriate.

6. If you go blank halfway through a conversation, play for time by using a filler phrase such as *eh bien, ce que je veux dire, en effet*, etc. Your French language assistant or teacher should be able to help you come up with an easy-to-learn list.

7. Don't say "ummm", say "euh". It sounds more French. Waving your arms about is very French too, but don't overdo it. You don't want to knock yourself out!

8. If you can't think of the word you want, use a word which refers to something similar, e.g. if you want to say: "I have lost my suitcase", but you can't remember the words for "lost" or "suitcase", you could say: *"Je ne peux pas trouver le sac où je mets mes vêtements quand je vais en vacances."*
Admittedly, this is not a sentence that will win any prizes in a short sentence competition, but it's better than saying nothing.

9. Be bold and ask for any question you didn't understand to be repeated. *"Voulez-vous répéter la question, s'il vous plaît?"* is the phrase you need. If after a second hearing you still haven't the foggiest what was asked, cut your losses, say: *"Je regrette, monsieur/madame, mais je ne comprends pas la question"*, and forget about it. Your future happiness does not rest on your reply to that one question.

188

How do you make French revision less boring?

9

It is a truth universally acknowledged that revising and chronic boredom are one and the same thing...

... but are they? OK, so if you were given the choice between revising for your final French exams and playing Twister with the celebrity of your choice, chances are you'd opt for the latter. But that doesn't mean French revision has to be a bore. The secret of a successful, non-boring French revision campaign is as follows:

1. Start revising well in advance of the exam. That way you can build plenty of fun-time into your revision schedule. Work out how you can best spread your revision over the time left before each exam – and yes, that includes the holidays. Even if your exam is nigh, this advice about spreading your revision over what time does remain is still sound.

2. Make sure you know the format of each exam (the ways in which the questions will be asked and what you are going to be examined on) so that you can plan your revision

accordingly. The two main areas your French revision should focus on are **a)** the different language skills and **b)** vocabulary and grammar.

3. Be a routine freak! Break your revision sessions down into one-hour blocks, with a short break in between, and a treat at the end of the session. (A cup of tea or a choccy biscuit, not a day out shopping!) Short, frequent breaks are a good idea because they help keep your brain as alert as possible and sometimes things that were driving you crazy before a break become much easier after one.

4. Vary what you revise. For example, instead of trying to learn vocabulary for an hour, spend around 10 minutes learning new words, followed by 10 minutes reading practice, followed by 10 minutes testing yourself on the same words, followed by 10 minutes speaking, followed by another 10 minutes re-testing yourself on the same words. By the end of the hour, you should be word perfect! *Fantastique!*

5. Alternate the skills that give you the most difficulty with those you find easier or more interesting. This will help stop you getting depressed and ensure you don't leave the skills or grammar you hate most until last.

Revision hit list – language skills

Here's a summary of various ways in which you can revise the different French language skills. For best results, use this revision hit list in conjunction with the tips above. (If you've just picked up this book and turned straight to this chapter, check out the earlier chapters too. There, you'll find many more details about what and how to revise.)

Reading

What to revise

- Identifying single words or phrases in a passage.
- Skim-reading to get the gist of a passage.

How to revise

- Re-do all the exercises you have covered in class.
- For extra practice, do the exercises in resources like Mary Glasgow magazines or *Etincelle* or any others your teacher might be able to suggest. Reading a French newspaper or magazine won't hurt you either.

Writing

What to revise

- Constructing sentences.
- Constructing passages.
- Formal/informal letters.
- Your writing checklists, i.e. the list of things you know you want to include in a piece of writing to make it impressive, and the list of errors you need to keep a look-out for in your work.

How to revise

- Re-read and re-do all the writing exercises your teacher has corrected.
- Familiarize yourself with vocabulary from your coursebook.
- Check out any rules of grammar you're not 100% sure about.

Listening

What to revise

- Picking out words and phrases in a passage.
- General listening to get an overall but accurate idea of what is being said.

How to revise

- Listen to resources which have a written copy of what's being said.
- Borrow tapes of exercises you have already done and have another go at them. Each time you listen you will hear more.
- Revise your vocab!

Speaking

What to revise

- Pronunciation and accent.
- Fluency, i.e. being able to say what you want to say at a reasonable speed and without too much hesitation.

How to revise

- Learn role-play expressions.
- Practise your general conversation topics and any presentation you have to give until you can do it in your sleep!
- Tape-record yourself speaking.
- Read aloud from any French text you can lay your hands on. This will help you get your tongue around French words more effectively.

Grammar SORTED

When it comes to grammar, these are the areas you need to revise in particular:

Verbs: Familiarize yourself with a variety of tenses.

Adjectives: As well as swotting up on the rules about gender and agreement, remind yourself how to make comparisons and how to say something is the best or worst.

Prepositions: Learn to use and recognize as many as you can.

Asking questions: Check you know how to!

Pronouns: Pay particular attention to the order they come in.

Making yourself concentrate properly on your revision isn't always easy, especially when you've got important daydreaming to do! One way you can help yourself to focus fully on your grammar revision is to write out each word or phrase you revise and then try to put it into a sentence. If you come across any point of grammar that you still can't get your head around, note it down and ask your teacher to go through it with you again.

(For hints and tips on learning/revising vocab, check out chapter 4.)

And so to the exam

How you feel in body and mind will have a big effect on how well you do in the different exams, so look after yourself and try to stay cheerful in the run-up to the big day. If you start to doubt your abilities, remind yourself that if you weren't considered up to the exam, your teacher wouldn't have entered you for it! If you find yourself getting fed up with the amount of work you have to do, think of the bigger picture; getting your French GCSE will take you one step nearer to getting a place at university or a great job and all that goes with it.

On the night before and day of each exam try to read, speak and listen to French only. That way you'll go into the exam room with your head crammed full of French. If you think it will help, pretend that you *are* French.

Remember to follow the exam tips given in chapters 5–8 as well.

Once an exam is over, don't re-live every *le* and *la*. Forget about it. Even if the worst comes to the worst and everything you feared might go pear-shaped has gone pear-shaped, it's not the end of the world. You can always put in for a re-sit: these things happen! Life goes on.

BONNE CHANCE!

Verbs

Regular verbs

Many French verbs are regular, i.e. they follow a set pattern.

On the following page you'll find a reminder of these set patterns. Regular verbs that end in **-er** in the infinitive follow the same pattern as *parler*. Regular verbs that end in **-ir** in the infinitive form follow the same pattern as *finir*. And regular verbs that end in **-re** in the infinitive follow the same pattern as *vendre*.

Reflexive verbs

Regular reflexive verbs are just like ordinary regular verbs except for two important differences.

1. They have an extra bit at the start that follows a simple pattern. (See *se laver* on page 197 to remind yourself what this pattern looks like.)

2. They use *être* in the perfect and pluperfect tenses.

Regular verbs

The *il* form is shown in the following table. The *elle* and *on* forms follow the same pattern unless shown separately. This also applies to *ils* and *elles*.

Infinitive	Present	Perfect	Imperfect	Pluperfect	Future	Conditional
parler	je parle	j'ai parlé	je parlais	j'avais parlé	je parlerai	je parlerais
to talk	tu parles	tu as parlé	tu parlais	tu avais parlé	tu parleras	tu parlerais
imperative	il parle	il a parlé	il parlait	il avait parlé	il parlera	il parlerait
parle!	nous parlons	nous avons parlé	nous parlions	nous avions parlé	nous parlerons	nous parlerions
parlons!	vous parlez	vous avez parlé	vous parliez	vous aviez parlé	vous parlerez	vous parleriez
parlez!	ils parlent	ils ont parlé	ils parlaient	ils avaient parlé	ils parleront	ils parleraient
finir	je finis	j'ai fini	je finissais	j'avais fini	je finirai	je finirais
to finish	tu finis	tu as fini	tu finissais	tu avais fini	tu finiras	tu finirais
imperative	il finit	il a fini	il finissait	il avait fini	il finira	il finirait
finis!	nous finissons	nous avons fini	nous finissions	nous avions fini	nous finirons	nous finirions
finissons!	vous finissez	vous avez fini	vous finissiez	vous aviez fini	vous finirez	vous finiriez
finissez!	ils finissent	ils ont fini	ils finissaient	ils avaient fini	ils finiront	ils finiraient
vendre	je vends	j'ai vendu	je vendais	j'avais vendu	je vendrai	je vendrais
to sell	tu vends	tu as vendu	tu vendais	tu avais vendu	tu vendras	tu vendrais
imperative	il vend	il a vendu	il vendait	il avait vendu	il vendra	il vendrait
vends!	nous vendons	nous avons vendu	nous vendions	nous avions vendu	nous vendrons	nous vendrions
vendons!	vous vendez	vous avez vendu	vous vendiez	vous aviez vendu	vous vendrez	vous vendriez
vendez!	ils vendent	ils ont vendu	ils vendaient	ils avaient vendu	ils vendront	ils vendraient

Regular verbs

Infinitive	Present	Perfect	Imperfect	Pluperfect	Future	Conditional
se laver *to wash oneself*	je me lave	je me suis lavé(e)	je me lavais	je m'étais lavé(e)	je me laverai	je me laverais
	tu te laves	tu t'es lavé(e)	tu te lavais	tu t'étais lavé(e)	tu te laveras	tu te laverais
	il se lave	il s'est lavé	il se lavait	il s'était lavé	il se lavera	il se laverait
		elle s'est lavée		elle s'était lavée		
	nous nous lavons	nous nous sommes lavé(e)s	nous nous lavions	nous nous étions lavé(e)s	nous nous laverons	nous nous laverions
	vous vous lavez	vous vous êtes lavé(e)(s)	vous vous laviez	vous vous étiez lavé(e)(s)	vous vous laverez	vous vous laveriez
	ils se lavent	ils se sont lavés	ils se lavaient	ils s'étaient lavés	ils se laveront	ils se laveraient
		elles se sont lavées		elles s'étaient lavées		
imperative lave-toi! lavons-nous! lavez-vous!						

Semi-regular verbs

The following **-er** verbs aren't really irregular but they do change their sound and spelling slightly in some tenses. Only the tenses where spelling changes apply are shown here. All other tenses are 100% regular.

acheter – to buy

Present	Future	Conditional
j'achète	j'achèterai	j'achèterais
tu achètes	tu achèteras	tu achèterais
il achète	il achètera	il achèterait
elle achète	elle achètera	elle achèterait
on achète	on achètera	on achèterait
nous achetons	nous achèterons	nous achèterions
vous achetez	vous achèterez	vous achèteriez
ils/elles achètent	ils/elles achèteront	ils/elles achèteraient

Other regular **-er** verbs that follow these spelling changes are *amener, mener, (se) lever, se promener* and *peser*.

espérer – to hope

Present
j'espère
tu espères
il/elle/on espère
nous espérons
vous espérez
ils/elles espèrent

Other regular **-er** verbs that follow these spelling changes are *s'inquiéter, préférer, protéger, répéter, (se) sécher, considérer*.

employer – to use

Present	Future	Conditional
j'emploie	j'emploierai	j'emploierais

tu emploies	tu emploieras	tu emploierais
il emploie	il emploiera	il emploierait
elle emploie	elle emploiera	elle emploierait
on emploie	on emploiera	on emploierait
nous employons	nous emploierons	nous emploierions
vous employez	vous emploierez	vous emploieriez
ils/elles emploient	ils/elles emploieront	ils/elles emploieraient

Other regular **-er** verbs that follow these spelling changes are *appuyer, essuyer, nettoyer, se noyer.*

appeler – to call

Present	Future	Conditional
j'appelle	j'appellerai	j'appellerais
tu appelles	tu appelleras	tu appellerais
il appelle	il appellera	il appellerait
elle appelle	elle appellera	elle appellerait
on appelle	on appellera	on appellerait
nous appelons	nous appellerons	nous appellerions
vous appelez	vous appellerez	vous appelleriez
ils/elles appellent	ils/elles appelleront	ils/elles apelleraient

Jeter, "to throw" works in the same way as *appeler* in that the **t** of *jeter* becomes **tt** in the same places that the **l** in *appeler* becomes **ll**.

manger – to eat

Present	Present participle	Imperfect
je mange	mangeant	je mangeais
tu manges		tu mangeais
il/elle/on mange		il/elle/on mangeait
nous mangeons		nous mangions
vous mangez		vous mangiez
ils/elles mangent		ils/elles mangeaient

All **-er** verbs in which the main part of the verb, or stem, ends in **-g-** work like *manger*.

lancer – to throw

Present	Present participle	Imperfect
je lance	lançant	je lançais
tu lances		tu lançais
il/elle/on lance		il/elle/on lançait
nous lançons		nous lancions
vous lancez		vous lanciez
ils/elles lancent		ils/elles lançaient

All **-er** verbs that have stems ending in **-c-** work like this.

Irregular verbs

For reasons best left unexplored, many of the most common French verbs are irregular, i.e. they do not follow the same pattern as their regular counterparts. This means you have to check them out one by one:

> **FANCY THAT!**
> Future endings for irregular verbs are the same as those for regular verbs. It's only the main part of the verb, or stem, that doesn't follow the usual rules in the future tense, e.g. *j'irai* – I will go.

(If you are ever unsure whether a verb is irregular or not, do check in your dictionary or ask your French teacher.)

Irregular verbs

The *elle* and *on* forms of the following verbs have the same pattern as the *il* form unless shown separately. This also applies to *ils* and *elles*. Check out pages 27 and 23 to see how the following verbs form the conditional and pluperfect tenses.

Infinitive	Present	Perfect	Imperfect	Future
aller *to go*	je vais tu vas il va	je suis <u>allé(e)</u> tu es allé(e) il est allé elle est allée	j'allais tu allais il allait	j'irai tu iras il ira
	nous allons vous allez ils vont	nous sommes allé(e)s vous êtes allé(e)(s) ils sont allés elles sont allées	nous allions vous alliez ils allaient	nous irons vous irez ils iront
imperative va! allons! allez!				
apprendre *to learn*	see **prendre**			
s'asseoir *to sit down*	je m'assieds tu t'assieds il s'assied	je me suis <u>assis(e)</u> tu t'es assis(e) il s'est assis elle s'est assise	je m'asseyais tu t'asseyais il s'asseyait	je m'assiérai tu t'assiéras il s'assiéra
	nous nous asseyons vous vous asseyez ils s'asseyent	nous nous sommes assis (e)s vous vous êtes assis(e)(s) ils se sont assis elles se sont assises	nous nous asseyions vous vous asseyiez ils s'asseyaient	nous nous assiérons vous vous assiérez ils s'assiéront
imperative assieds-toi! asseyons-nous! asseyez-vous!				

201

Irregular verbs

Infinitive	Present	Perfect	Imperfect	Future
avoir	j'ai	j'ai eu	j'avais	j'aurai
to have	tu as	tu as eu	tu avais	tu auras
imperative	il a	il a eu	il avait	il aura
aie!	nous avons	nous avons eu	nous avions	nous aurons
ayons!	vous avez	vous avez eu	vous aviez	vous aurez
avez!	ils ont	ils ont eu	ils avaient	ils auront
boire	je bois	j'ai bu	je buvais	je boirai
to drink	tu bois	tu as bu	tu buvais	tu boiras
imperative	il boit	il a bu	il buvait	il boira
bois!	nous buvons	nous avons bu	nous buvions	nous boirons
buvons!	vous buvez	vous avez bu	vous buviez	vous boirez
buvez!	ils boivent	ils ont bu	ils buvaient	ils boiront
comprendre	see **prendre**			
to understand				
conduire	je conduis	j'ai conduit	je conduisais	je conduirai
to drive	tu conduis	tu as conduit	tu conduisais	tu conduiras
imperative	il conduit	il a conduit	il conduisait	il conduira
conduis!	nous conduisons	nous avons conduit	nous conduisions	nous conduirons
conduisons!	vous conduisez	vous avez conduit	vous conduisiez	vous conduirez
conduisez!	ils conduisent	ils ont conduit	ils conduisaient	ils conduiront

202

connaître
to know
imperative
connais!
connaissons!
connaissez!

je connais	j'ai connu	je connaissais	je connaîtrai
tu connais	tu as connu	tu connaissais	tu connaîtras
il connaît	il a connu	il connaissait	il connaîtra
nous connaissons	nous avons connu	nous connaissions	nous connaîtrons
vous connaissez	vous avez connu	vous connaissiez	vous connaîtrez
ils connaissent	ils ont connu	ils connaissaient	ils connaîtront

courir
to run
imperative
cours!
courons!
courez!

je cours	j'ai couru	je courais	je courrai
tu cours	tu as couru	tu courais	tu courras
il court	il a couru	il courait	il courra
nous courons	nous avons couru	nous courions	nous courrons
vous courez	vous avez couru	vous couriez	vous courrez
ils courent	ils ont couru	ils couraient	ils courront

croire
to believe,
to think
imperative
crois!
croyons!
croyez!

je crois	j'ai cru	je croyais	je croirai
tu crois	tu as cru	tu croyais	tu croiras
il croit	il a cru	il croyait	il croira
nous croyons	nous avons cru	nous croyions	nous croirons
vous croyez	vous avez cru	vous croyiez	vous croirez
ils croient	ils ont cru	ils croyaient	ils croiront

devoir
to have to
imperative
dois!
devons!
devez!

je dois	j'ai dû	je devais	je devrai
tu dois	tu as dû	tu devais	tu devras
il doit	il a dû	il devait	il devra
nous devons	nous avons dû	nous devions	nous devrons
vous devez	vous avez dû	vous deviez	vous devrez
ils doivent	ils ont dû	ils devaient	ils devront

Irregular verbs

Infinitive	Present	Perfect	Imperfect	Future
dire				
to say	je dis	j'ai dit	je disais	je dirai
imperative	tu dis	tu as dit	tu disais	tu diras
dis!	il dit	il a dit	il disait	il dira
disons!	nous disons	nous avons dit	nous disions	nous dirons
dites!	vous dites	vous avez dit	vous disiez	vous direz
	ils disent	ils ont dit	ils disaient	ils diront
dormir				
to sleep	je dors	j'ai dormi	je dormais	je dormirai
imperative	tu dors	tu as dormi	tu dormais	tu dormiras
dors!	il dort	il a dormi	il dormait	il dormira
dormons!	nous dormons	nous avons dormi	nous dormions	nous dormirons
dormez!	vous dormez	vous avez dormi	vous dormiez	vous dormirez
	ils dorment	ils ont dormi	ils dormaient	ils dormiront
écrire				
to write	j'écris	j'ai écrit	j'écrivais	j'écrirai
imperative	tu écris	tu as écrit	tu écrivais	tu écriras
écris!	il écrit	il a écrit	il écrivait	il écrira
écrivons!	nous écrivons	nous avons écrit	nous écrivions	nous écrirons
écrivez!	vous écrivez	vous avez écrit	vous écriviez	vous écririez
	ils écrivent	ils ont écrit	ils écrivaient	ils écriront
envoyer				
to send	j'envoie	j'ai envoyé	j'envoyais	j'enverrai
imperative	tu envoies	tu as envoyé	tu envoyais	tu enverras
envoie!	il envoie	il a envoyé	il envoyait	il enverra
envoyons!	nous envoyons	nous avons envoyé	nous envoyions	nous enverrons
envoyez!	vous envoyez	vous avez envoyé	vous envoyiez	vous enverrez
	ils envoient	ils ont envoyé	ils envoyaient	ils enverront

essayer — *to try*
imperative: essaie! essayons! essayez!

	Present	Passé composé	Imperfect	Future
	j'essaie	j'ai <u>essayé</u>	j'essayais	j'essaierai
	tu essaies	tu as essayé	tu essayais	tu essaieras
	il essaie	il a essayé	il essayait	il essaiera
	nous essayons	nous avons essayé	nous essayions	nous essaierons
	vous essayez	vous avez essayé	vous essayiez	vous essaierez
	ils essaient	ils ont essayé	ils essayaient	ils essaieront

être — *to be*
imperative: sois! soyons! soyez!

	Present	Passé composé	Imperfect	Future
	je suis	j'ai <u>été</u>	j'étais	je serai
	tu es	tu as été	tu étais	tu seras
	il est	il a été	il était	il sera
	nous sommes	nous avons été	nous étions	nous serons
	vous êtes	vous avez été	vous étiez	vous serez
	ils sont	ils ont été	ils étaient	ils seront

faire — *to do, make*
imperative: fais! faisons! faites!

	Present	Passé composé	Imperfect	Future
	je fais	j'ai <u>fait</u>	je faisais	je ferai
	tu fais	tu as fait	tu faisais	tu feras
	il fait	il a fait	il faisait	il fera
	nous faisons	nous avons fait	nous faisions	nous ferons
	vous faites	vous avez fait	vous faisiez	vous ferez
	ils font	ils ont fait	ils faisaient	ils feront

falloir — *must, is necessary*

	Present	Passé composé	Imperfect	Future
	il faut	il a <u>fallu</u>	il fallait	il faudra

se lever — *to get up*
imperative: lève-toi! levons-nous! levez-vous!

	Present	Passé composé	Imperfect	Future
	je me lève	je me suis <u>levé(e)</u>	je me levais	je me lèverai
	tu te lèves	tu t'es levé(e)	tu te levais	tu te lèveras
	il se lève	il s'est levé	il se levait	il se lèvera
		elle s'est levée		
	nous nous levons	nous nous sommes levé(e)s	nous nous levions	nous nous lèverons
	vous vous levez	vous vous êtes levé(e)(s)	vous vous leviez	vous vous lèverez
	ils se lèvent	ils se sont levés	ils se levaient	ils se lèveront
		elles se sont levées		

205

Irregular verbs

Infinitive	Present	Perfect	Imperfect	Future
lire	je lis	j'ai lu	je lisais	je lirai
to read	tu lis	tu as lu	tu lisais	tu liras
imperative	il lit	il a lu	il lisait	il lira
lis!	nous lisons	nous avons lu	nous lisions	nous lirons
lisons!	vous lisez	vous avez lu	vous lisiez	vous lirez
lisez!	ils lisent	ils ont lu	ils lisaient	ils liront
mettre	je mets	j'ai mis	je mettais	je mettrai
to put, put on	tu mets	tu as mis	tu mettais	tu mettras
imperative	il met	il a mis	il mettait	il mettra
mets!	nous mettons	nous avons mis	nous mettions	nous mettrons
mettons!	vous mettez	vous avez mis	vous mettiez	vous mettrez
mettez!	ils mettent	ils ont mis	ils mettaient	ils mettront
mourir	je meurs	je suis mort(e)	je mourais	je mourrai
to die	tu meurs	tu es mort(e)	tu mourais	tu mourras
imperative	il meurt	il est mort	il mourait	il mourra
meurs!		elle est morte		
mourons!	nous mourons	nous sommes mort(e)s	nous mourions	nous mourrons
mourez!	vous mourez	vous êtes mort(e)(s)	vous mouriez	vous mourrez
	ils meurent	ils sont morts	ils mouraient	ils mourront
		elles sont mortes		

naître
to be born

je nais
tu nais
il naît
nous naissons
vous naissez
ils naissent

je suis né(e)
tu es né(e)
il est né
elle est née
nous sommes né(e)s
vous êtes né(e)(s)
ils sont nés
elles sont nées

je naissais
tu naissais
il naissait
nous naissions
vous naissiez
ils naissaient

je naîtrai
tu naîtras
il naîtra
nous naîtrons
vous naîtrez
ils naîtront

ouvrir
to open
imperative
ouvre!
ouvrons!
ouvrez!

j'ouvre
tu ouvres
il ouvre
nous ouvrons
vous ouvrez
ils ouvrent

j'ai ouvert
tu as ouvert
il a ouvert
nous avons ouvert
vous avez ouvert
ils ont ouvert

j'ouvrais
tu ouvrais
il ouvrait
nous ouvrions
vous ouvriez
ils ouvraient

j'ouvrirai
tu ouvriras
il ouvrira
nous ouvrirons
vous ouvrirez
ils ouvriront

partir
to leave, depart
imperative
pars!
partons!
partez!

je pars
tu pars
il part
nous partons
vous partez
ils partent

je suis parti(e)
tu es parti(e)
il est parti
elle est partie
nous sommes parti(e)(s)
vous êtes parti(e)(s)
ils sont partis
elles sont parties

je partais
tu partais
il partait
nous partions
vous partiez
ils partaient

je partirai
tu partiras
il partira
nous partirons
vous partirez
ils partiront

Irregular verbs

Infinitive	Present	Perfect	Imperfect	Future
pleuvoir *to rain*	il pleut	il a <u>plu</u>	il pleuvait	il pleuvra
pouvoir *to be able* (I can etc.)	je peux tu peux il peut nous pouvons vous pouvez ils peuvent	j'ai <u>pu</u> tu as pu il a pu nous avons pu vous avez pu ils ont pu	je pouvais tu pouvais il pouvait nous pouvions vous pouviez ils pouvaient	je pourrai tu pourras il pourra nous pourrons vous pourrez ils pourront
prendre *to take* **imperative** prends! prenons! prenez!	je prends tu prends il prend nous prenons vous prenez ils prennent	j'ai <u>pris</u> tu as pris il a pris nous avons pris vous avez pris ils ont pris	je prenais tu prenais il prenait nous prenions vous preniez ils prenaient	je prendrai tu prendras il prendra nous prendrons vous prendrez ils prendront
recevoir *to receive* **imperative** reçois! recevons! recevez!	je reçois tu reçois il reçoit nous recevons vous recevez ils reçoivent	j'ai <u>reçu</u> tu as reçu il a reçu nous avons reçu vous avez reçu ils ont reçu	je recevais tu recevais il recevait nous recevions vous receviez ils recevaient	je recevrai tu recevras il recevra nous recevrons vous recevrez ils recevront

208

rire
to laugh
imperative
ris!
rions!
riez!

je ris
tu ris
il rit
nous rions
vous riez
ils rient

j'ai ri
tu as ri
il a ri
nous avons ri
vous avez ri
ils ont ri

je riais
tu riais
il riait
nous riions
vous riiez
ils riaient

je rirai
tu riras
il rira
nous rirons
vous rirez
ils riront

savoir
to know
imperative
sache!
sachons!
sachez!

je sais
tu sais
il sait
nous savons
vous savez
ils savent

j'ai su
tu as su
il a su
nous avons su
vous avez su
ils ont su

je savais
tu savais
il savait
nous savions
vous saviez
ils savaient

je saurai
tu sauras
il saura
nous saurons
vous saurez
ils sauront

sortir
to go out

see **partir**

tenir
to hold

see **venir**, but note: **tenir** uses 'avoir' in the perfect and pluperfect tenses.

venir
to come
imperative
viens!
venons!
venez!

je viens
tu viens
il vient
nous venons
vous venez
ils viennent

je suis venu(e)
tu es venu(e)
il est venu
elle est venue
nous sommes venu(e)s
vous êtes venu(e)(s)
ils sont venus
elles sont venues

je venais
tu venais
il venait
nous venions
vous veniez
ils venaient

je viendrai
tu viendras
il viendra
nous viendrons
vous viendrez
ils viendront

Irregular verbs

Infinitive	Present	Perfect	Imperfect	Future
vivre	je vis	j'ai vécu	je vivais	je vivrai
to live	tu vis	tu as vécu	tu vivais	tu vivras
imperative	il vit	il a vécu	il vivait	il vivra
vis!	nous vivons	nous avons vécu	nous vivions	nous vivrons
vivons!	vous vivez	vous avez vécu	vous viviez	vous vivrez
vivez!	ils vivent	ils ont vécu	ils vivaient	ils vivront
voir	je vois	j'ai vu	je voyais	je verrai
to see	tu vois	tu as vu	tu voyais	tu verras
imperative	il voit	il a vu	il voyait	il verra
vois!	nous voyons	nous avons vu	nous voyions	nous verrons
voyons!	vous voyez	vous avez vu	vous voyiez	vous verrez
voyez!	ils voient	ils ont vu	ils voyaient	ils verront
vouloir	je veux	j'ai voulu	je voulais	je voudrai
to want	tu veux	tu as voulu	tu voulais	tu voudras
imperative	il veut	il a voulu	il voulait	il voudra
veuille!	nous voulons	nous avons voulu	nous voulions	nous voudrons
veuillons!	vous voulez	vous avez voulu	vous vouliez	vous voudrez
veuillez!	ils veulent	ils ont voulu	ils voulaient	ils voudront

Note: *devenir* and *revenir* follow the same pattern as *venir*, *disparaître* – the same pattern as *connaître*, etc.

210

> **FANCY THAT!**
> All **-oir** verbs are irregular.

"ADVENT" verbs

The verbs below, which can be remembered by the word ADVENT, form the first part of the perfect and pluperfect tenses with *être*. NB: Past participles are in brackets.

Aller (allé)	to go	arriver (arrivé)	to arrive	The two As
Descendre (descendu)	to go down	monter (monté)	to go up	
Venir (venu)	to come	partir (parti)	to leave	The four pairs of opposites
Entrer (entré)	to enter	sortir (sorti)	to go out	
Naitre (né)	to be born	mourir (mort)	to die	
Tomber (tombé)	to fall	rester (resté)	to stay	The two left over!

Verbs and reflexives built up from these verbs also use *être* in the perfect and pluperfect tenses, e.g. *rentrer* – to come back; *devenir* – to become.

Answers

Chapter 1: What did you say a verb was?
Page 32
1. *regardais, a téléphoné, voulait, prenait, est sortie, a mis, a répondu, a dit, allait, avait, a vu, étais, était, a invité.*

If you don't understand why these tenses were used in the answers to question one, read on . . .

regardais – "I was watching", i.e. the action was happening, so the imperfect tense is needed (see page 21).

a téléphoné – "he telephoned", i.e. this action happened once, so the perfect tense is needed (see page 16).

voulait – "he wanted", i.e. he didn't just want for a minute and then stop wanting, making the action complete, oh no: this was an ongoing state he was in, so the imperfect tense is needed (see page 21).

prenait – "she was taking", so the imperfect tense is needed (see page 21).

est sortie – "she got out", i.e. this was a single action that happened once, so the perfect tense is needed (see page 16).

Because the perfect tense of *sortir* is formed with *être* not *avoir*, and because the person doing the getting out is female, *sorti* has an -e on the end.

a mis – "she put on", i.e. this was a single action that happened once, so the perfect tense is needed (see page 16). *Mis* is the past participle of *mettre* (see irregular verb list on page 206).

a répondu – "she answered", i.e. this was a single action that happened once, so the perfect tense is needed (see page 16).

a dit – "he said", i.e. this was a single action that happened once, so the perfect tense is needed (see page 16).

allait – "he was going". The word "was" lets you know that the imperfect tense is needed (see page 21).

avait – "he had". Like *voulait* above, he didn't suddenly stop having a lot of work, the "lot of work" was ongoing so the imperfect tense is needed (see page 21).

a vu – "she saw", i.e. this action happened once and is finished, so the perfect tense is needed (see page 16).

étais – "I was". Like *voulait* above, the speaker didn't suddenly stop being disappointed, he was in an ongoing state of disappointment, so the imperfect tense is needed (see page 21).

était – "it was", i.e. his birthday was taking place so the imperfect tense is needed (see page 21).

a invité – "she invited". This particular action happened once and is finished, so the perfect tense is needed (see page 16).

2. *aurai, achètera, donneront, irons, ferons, sera, aura, pourra, téléphonera.*

3. *achèterais, ferais, visiterais, inviterais, nous amuserions, recevraient, aurait, voudrait.*

4. *je suis allé(e), j'y suis resté(e), j'ai eu, c' était, j'ai vu, il y avait, jouaient, dansaient, chantaient, il y avait.*

The answers to **4.** explained:

je suis allé(e) and *j'y suis resté(e)* – "I went", "I stayed there". Both are actions that happened and are complete so the perfect tense is needed. You need only have added the extra -e if you had decided that the person talking about Martinique was female.

j'ai eu – "I had". The perfect is the correct tense here but if you put *j'avais* that's OK too, even though it gives a slightly different meaning.

c'était – "it was". The word "was" lets you know that the imperfect tense is needed.

j'ai vu – "I saw". The action is complete so the perfect tense is needed.

il y avait – "there were". Like the word "was", "were" lets you know that the imperfect tense is needed.

jouaient, dansaient, chantaient – "were playing", "were dancing", "were singing". The playing, dancing and singing were ongoing at that time so the imperfect is used.

il y avait – "there was". See above.

5. *s'était inspiré, avait gagné, étaient allés.*

Translations

1. I was watching television when my father telephoned. He wanted to speak to my mother. As she was having a bath she got out quickly, put on a dressing gown and answered the telephone. My father said that he was going to be back late because he had a lot of work. My mother saw that I was disappointed because it was my birthday. So she invited me out to the restaurant.

2. Tomorrow, I will be 17 years old. My mother will buy a big chocolate cake! My friends will give me lots of presents. In the afternoon, we will go to the cinema and in the evening we will have a big party at my house. That will be great. All my friends will be there! The only problem is Marc. He won't be able to come because he's working, but he will phone me, he promised.

3. If I were very rich, I would buy a big house with a swimming pool. I would go around the world. I would visit as many countries as possible and I would invite my friends. We would have a lot of fun. My parents would receive a car as a present and my little sister would have all the toys she could wish for.

4. Last year I went to Martinique. I stayed there for three weeks. I was lucky because it was carnival time. I saw all the parades. There were people everywhere. The bands played fantastic music. People were dancing and singing. There was a great atmosphere.

5.
- To direct his film, *The Big Blue*, the director Luc Besson had taken his inspiration from the exploits of the famous French diver, Jacques Mayol.
- If only the English team had won the 1998 World Cup!
- William and Wilma said that they had gone to the disco with their friends.

215

Chapter 2: I can't make sense of French sentences!
Page 40
1. *passage, moitié.*

2. *des oiseaux, des animaux, des fils, des voix, des feux, des pneus, des œufs, des plages.*

3.

Salut

*Je m'appelle Jackie. J'ai quinze ans et j'adore regarder **la** télé tous les jours. Mon émission préférée c'est **un** feuilleton. C'est **l'**histoire de plusieurs familles à Manchester. **Les** familles passent beaucoup de temps dans un bar. Quelle vie!*

*Hier matin ma télé est tombée en panne donc je suis allée en ville. J'ai rencontré **des** amies et nous avons fait les magasins. J'ai acheté **du** parfum et ma meilleure amie a acheté **de la** crème pour les mains et **de l'**huile solaire.*

*Tu peux m'envoyer **une** photo de toi?*

À bientôt.

Jackie

Page 45

Cher Jacques,

*Me voici en vacances à Bognor Regis. Hier, j'ai fait la connaissance d'une **jolie** jeune femme qui s'appelle Monica. Elle a les cheveux **bruns** et les yeux **bleus** et les pieds **parfaits.** Ensemble, on a visité la **vieille** ville ce matin. Après cela, nous sommes allés au cinéma et nous avons regardé un long film **anglais** sans sous-titres que je ne pouvais pas comprendre. La grammaire **anglaise** me semble très difficile. Si seulement j'étais bilingue!*

À bientôt,

Matt

216

Dear Jacques,

Here I am on holiday in Bognor Regis. Yesterday I met a pretty young woman called Monica. She has brown hair and blue eyes and perfect feet. We visited the old town together this morning. After that, we went to the cinema and watched a long English film without subtitles, which I couldn't understand. English grammar seems very difficult to me. If only I were bilingual!

See you soon,

Matt

Page 48

1. a) Unless your mother is in the habit of wearing fried eggs, in which case **c)**.

2. b) And thank your lucky lemons the girl/boy of your dreams was not on hand to witness your brother's performance.

3. c) The bloke in question fell out with Steven Spielberg years ago.

4. c) Unless you've just won the lottery, in which case **b)**. Expensive French restaurants are very expensive.

5. b) Unless the cat had massive gambling debts, in which case **a)** and **b)**.

Page 53

1.

A	B
toujours	jamais
vite	lentement
très	peu
souvent	rarement
heureusement	malheureusement
gentiment	cruellement

2. Hier soir, Jean Julliano, le créateur branché de la haute couture française, est mort dans un accident de moto à Walton-on-the-

Naze. Bien que les circonstances exactes de l'accident ne soient pas entièrement claires, il ne fait aucun doute que Monsieur Julliano avait conduit trop **vite**.

3.
- Je fais toujours la vaisselle.
- Nous avons déjà visité la France.
- Bertha fumait beaucoup.
- Le camping, c'est bien pour la santé.
- Les enfants savent parler anglais très couramment.
- Elle est bientôt devenue une vedette sensationnelle.
- Il travaille seulement une heure le soir.

Page 58
1.
- Les fromages de France sont les meilleurs.
- Tu chantes mieux/vous chantez mieux.
- Je voudrais un meilleur vélo.
- Là-bas, c'est pire.
- Avez-vous quelque chose de moins cher?/As-tu quelque chose de moins cher?
- Le hand est moins difficile que les maths.
- Je préfère le rugby parce que c'est plus intéressant que le football.

Page 59
2.
1. Faux. L'Espagne n'est pas aussi grande que la France/La France est plus grande que l'Espagne/L'Espagne est moins grande que la France. (La France est le pays le plus grand de Europe de l'Ouest.)

2. Vrai. Paris-ville est plus petit que Greater London. (Paris-ville est à peu près 15 fois plus petit que Greater London.)

3. Vrai. La religion la plus populaire de la France, c'est le catholicisme.

4. Faux. Une baguette française mesure plus longue que 50 centimètres.

218

(Une baguette française mesure environ 80 centimètres.)

5. *Faux. La cité la plus grande de la France, ce n'est pas Marseilles.*
(La cité la plus grande de la France, c'est Paris.)

6. *Faux. La Loire est plus longue que la Seine/La Seine n'est pas aussi*
longue que la Loire/La Seine est moins longue que la Loire.
(La Loire mesure 1,010 km et la Seine mesure 770 km.)

7. *Vrai. "La Comédie Française" à Paris est le théâtre le plus célèbre*
de la France.

8. *Vrai. Le français est parlé par plus de 200 millions de personnes du*
monde.

Page 66
1.
- *L'été prochain, je vais passer mes vacances avec ma tante.*
- *Hier soir Charlie est allé au restaurant avec ses parents et sa*
cousine, Bella.
- *Il fait toujours ses devoirs dans leur chambre.*
- *Nos matières préférées sont l'anglais et le dessin.*
- *Hier elle est allée au cinéma parce que c'était l'anniversaire de sa*
meilleure amie, Jane.

2. *ce soir, cette robe, ce collant, ces chaussures, cette veste, celle-ci,*
celui-ci, celui-là.

Page 76
- *Les boy bands? Je les adore.*
- *La directrice veut nous voir cet après-midi.*
- *Je lui ai offert une nouvelle voiture.*
- *Il me le donne.*
- *Les lettres des garçons? Nous les leur enverrons.*
- *Les prix? Il nous les a présentés.*

Page 76
What Madame A. should have asked was: *"Vous la lui avez vendue?"* not *"Vous lui l'avez vendue?"*

Page 88
- *La paire de baskets est sous l'armoire.*
- *Le jean en cuir est dans l'armoire.*
- *Les CDs sont près de la chaîne-stéréo.*
- *Le téléphone est sur la table.*
- *Les magasins du football sont par terre.*
- *Le journal est derrière les rideaux.*
- *La vidéocassette de Keith Chegwin est devant la lampe.*

Page 94
1. The first one. He obviously can't be a true Frenchman because he has replied to your question in the wrong tense. When you reply in French, you should always mirror the tense of the question you are asked.

2. Your third question is the trick one because you have made the common mistake of trying to translate the English "do" in "Do you live in Paris?" A true Frenchman/woman would have said: *"Habitez-vous à Paris?"* or *"Est-ce que vous habitez à Paris?"*
You know that Fifi Fou-Fou must be English because:
a) she didn't spot your deliberate error.
b) she repeated the same error in her answer.
c) no self-respecting Frenchwoman would call herself Fifi Fou-Fou.

Page 98
- *J'aime beaucoup mon meilleur ami parce qu'il est rigolo.*
- *J'aime me bronzer quand il fait beau.*
- *Nous sommes entrés dans un café où nous avons mangé un repas délicieux.*
- *Ma chambre est grande avec une fenêtre qui donne sur la rue.*
- *Je suis allé(e) voir ma tante qui habitait tout près.*

- *Hier j'ai eu un accident qui était assez grave.*
- *Je n'aime pas ça!*
- *Elle n'est pas allée en ville ce soir.*
- *Je n'oublierai jamais cette boum.*
- *Demain je ne vais rien faire!*

Chapter 3: Dictionaries drive me demented!

Page 104

Mesdames, messieurs, bijoux, choux, châteaux, feux, bureaux, mesdemoiselles, yeux.

(lady) and (gentleman), there is a thief in our village! Yesterday he stole some (jewel) and some (cabbage) from the two (stately home) on the hill and today he stole the (traffic light) in front of the (office) of (miss) Collette and Claire. I beg you to keep your (eye) open and to look for this thief. If you see him, let the police know.

Chapter 5: Read any good French lately?

Page 126

a) Unless you're a lazy slob, in which case **c)**. The Metro car, like all other cars in French, is feminine, but *le Métro*, as in the underground railway, is masculine. So, now you know!

Page 135

1. *Les enfants et les personnes âgées.*

2. *Des centaines.*

3. *Plus de 200.*

4. *On doit bien cuire les aliments.*

5. *Le poulet, les œufs et les glaces.* (If you put another food made with raw eggs instead of "*les glaces*", you still get your three marks.)

Page 137

1. Someone who takes drugs regularly and is dependent on them.

2. Any three of these reasons would be correct: curiosity/pressure from their friends/to forget their problems or find a way of escape from their problems/to combat stress.

3. Any three of these answers would be correct: hallucinations/suffocation/coma/brain haemorrhage (bleeding)/ heart attack.

4. They have a higher risk of getting AIDS or hepatitis.

5. They can cause accidents that can be fatal.

Chapter 7: How do you write right in French?
Page 153

1. Possible answers
   a) *C'était super*
   b) *C'est délicieux*
   c) *Ce sera intéressant*
   d) *C'était affreux*

2. Possible answers
   a) *J'adore la biologie parce que je suis fort(e) en biologie.*
   b) *Je déteste l'anglais parce que je ne suis pas fort(e) en anglais.*
   c) *Je préfère passer les grandes vacances dans un pays chaud parce que j'aime bien me bronzer.*
   d) *Je voudrais travailler dans une confiserie parce que j'adore les bons-bons.*

3. *L'été dernier j'ai travaillé dans un supermarché qui était près du*

centre-ville. C'était affreux et je n'ai pas gagné beaucoup d'argent.

L'été prochain j'irai en France et je travaillerai dans un café. J'ai déjà été en France et j'ai vraiment aimé mes vacances là-bas.

En ce moment je révise pour mes examens. J'ai beaucoup de devoirs et je n'aime pas ça. Le weekend dernier, par exemple, je suis resté(e) dans ma chambre et j'ai passé tout mon temps à travailler. Je me suis tellement ennuyé(e)!

Page 162
1.
Cher ami,
Tu me demandes ce que j'ai fait ce matin. Comme d'habitude je me suis levé(e) à sept heures et demie, je me suis lavé(e) et je me suis habillé(e). Avant de quitter la maison, j'ai pris le petit déjeuner – du thé et du pain grillé. Après avoir mangé, je suis sorti(e) pour aller prendre le train à l'école.

En arrivant à l'école, j'ai rencontré mon ami, Joey, et nous avons bavardé pendant quelques minutes. Notre première leçon a commencé à neuf heures précises. C'était assez intéressante!

Et toi, que fais-tu le matin quand tu vas à l'école? Est-ce que tu dois te lever tôt? Samedi prochain, je vais rester au lit toute la journée!
Écris-moi vite.

2.
- Je n'ai jamais visité le Brésil mais j'aimerais bien y aller un jour.
- J'habite à Birmingham depuis quinze ans et j'aime y habiter.
- Nous avons été en Ecosse il y a deux ans et c'était superbe!
- J'étais en train de garer la voiture quand une ambulance est entrée en collision avec la vieille femme.
- Il y a eu un accident! Y a-t-il un médecin ici?
- Combien de films d'épouvante est-ce que tu as vu? J'en ai vu vingt-neuf!

Page 169
The eleven *erreurs affreuses* have been corrected below:

Leeds, le 6 mars 2001

Madame/Monsieur,
J'ai l'intention de passer quelques jours à Nice au mois de septembre. **Avez**-vous **une** chambre libre du 1 au 4 septembre? Je voudrais réserver **une grande** chambre pour une personne avec mini-bar. **J'ai** un **vieux** chien. Vous **permettez** aux **animaux** de loger dans votre hôtel?
   On m'a **dit** que les restaurants dans l'hôtel sont **les meilleurs** de Nice. **C'est** vrai? Et le chef, préparera-t-il des repas pour les animaux?
   Je vous prie d'agréer, Madame/Monsieur, l'expression de mes sentiments distingués.

Wally Weeve

Page 169

Model letter:

Leeds, le 6 mars 2001

Madame/Monsieur,
J'ai l'intention de passer quelques jours à Nice au mois d'avril. Avez-vous une chambre libre du 12 au 14 avril? Je voudrais réserver une chambre pour deux personnes avec douche. J'ai un vieux chien. Vous permettez aux animaux de loger dans votre hôtel?
   On m'a dit que les restaurants dans l'hôtel sont les meilleurs de Nice. C'est vrai? Le dîner commence à quelle heure, s'il vous plaît?
   Je vous prie d'agréer, Madame/Monsieur, l'expression de mes sentiments distingués.

Wally Weeve